A doctor's personal journey
through anorexia

Dr ght
with rd

malcolm down

PUBLISHING

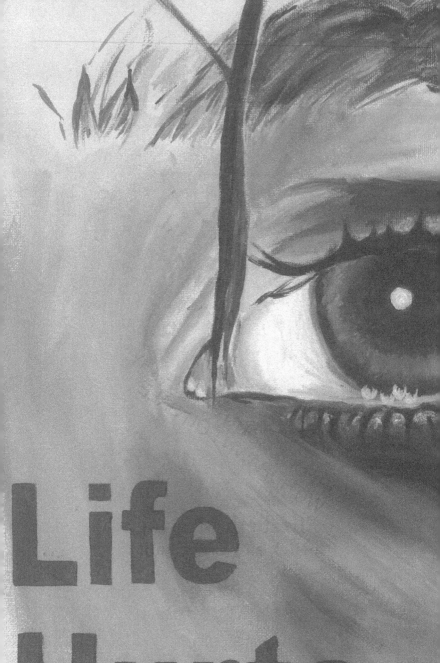

When I was sixteen years old, and seeking a way through anorexia, I painted a picture of my own eye and added the words 'Life Hurts' to express my feelings. Little did I know that this would later become the title of a book. But that phrase continued to be very important to me as I battled against the illness and became a doctor. The fact is that everyone experiences hurts, and everyone hurts others, but we can find a hope and a future for our own lives, which we can share with others.

21 20 19 18 17 16   7 6 5 4 3 2 1

First published 2017 by Malcolm Down Publishing Ltd.
www.malcolmdown.co.uk

British Library Cataloguing in Publication Data
A catalogue record for this book is available from the British Library.

ISBN 978-1-910786-65-9

Cover design by William Montout.
Photography: Abigail Cole (The Cole Portfolio Photography)
and Carol Pollard.

Printed in the UK

I Know a Girl

I know a girl
Whose life is a lie
She sets herself targets
Never asks herself why

I know a girl
Who's tired and weak
She stutters and trembles
And struggles to speak

I know a girl
Who hates what she sees
She tries to improve
Is eager to please

I know a girl
Who's not sure who to be
She's desperate and lonely
This girl is me

I wrote this poem in January 2007, when I was fourteen years old, in-between an emergency admission to general hospital and my time at a long-stay inpatient hospital.

Contents

Foreword

I feel honoured to write a foreword to Dr McNaught's book on behalf of the Royal College of Psychiatrists Faculty of Eating Disorders. She speaks so bravely about her personal experiences, both as a patient and as a doctor. I met Lizzie at the Faculty of Eating Disorders annual conference in November 2016. That day her speech got a standing ovation from the professionals, who were deeply moved by her message. She has a clear voice, both when she speaks and when she writes. She is passionate about improving services for patients with eating disorders and improving the training of doctors.

In her writing, she moves from the position of a professional looking at herself through her medical knowledge to that of a person caught in struggles against an eating disorder. I wondered if it can sometimes blur the reality that "This girl is me". Doctors speak about insight, being able to make sense of your experiences of mental health difficulties. Insight can be elusive to even the most able and gifted of professionals. Lizzie calls it getting a perspective.

I would recommend this book to patients with eating disorders and their families. I would also recommend it to professionals and doctors learning to practice as health professionals. Lizzie took great care to explain symptoms of anorexia nervosa both objectively as defined by professionals and subjectively, exactly how they felt to her. This is unique, as Lizzie is both a patient and a doctor. Her vantage point makes this book a useful educational tool. Lizzie offers a fresh look at the similarities between mental illness and physical ones. She compares treating anorexia nervosa with therapy to treating pneumonia with antibiotics.

Lizzie describes professionals she has met on her journey in kind and appreciative words. Some of them were struggling with the limitations of their knowledge and understanding of anorexia nervosa and those encounters were missed opportunities to overcome the illness.

Within the Faculty, we share Lizzie's wish that eating disorders are afforded a more prominent place in the medical undergraduate curriculum and that there is more training on the subject to all health professionals. From research on the subject we know that most medical students know someone with an eating disorder and most of them feel that there should be more teaching on this illness, which can seriously affect the health of young people.

Our patients, seemingly caught in the grip of anorexia nervosa are grappling with much bigger issues. They are growing into their own skin, individuating into a unique person, accepting who they are. On that level Lizzie's book is for everyone. Those struggles and the fact that life hurts are universal

Dr Izabela Jurewicz MRCPsych, MSci, LMSSA
Educational Lead
Faculty of Eating Disorders
Royal College of Psychiatrists

Preface

I am telling my story, and reflecting upon it from my perspective as a doctor, in the hope that this will inspire and encourage others to see that, although life hurts, there is hope for all of us.

Everyone has regrets. Probably, all of us wish that we could speak to ourselves in the past. So, after each chapter I will include a 'letter to myself at that time'. I hope that this will help others in a similar situation.

Many other people have shared this journey with me, especially my dad and mum, Nick and Carol Pollard, who have helped me to write this book. They have also provided valuable insights from their perspectives which I have included in the appendix. I hope that these will be useful for families, friends and others who are seeking to help people on their own journey through anorexia.

Also in the appendix is some information on the signs and symptoms of anorexia, its impact on families, and some ways to find help. Most important is a 'letter to someone going to see the doctor', because that first appointment has so much potential to save people from the ravages of this dreadful disease (this is also available as a download from LifeHurts.net).

Finally, a word about terminology. Technically there is a difference between 'anorexia' and 'anorexia nervosa'. Strictly speaking, anorexia simply refers to a loss of appetite which could have multiple causes (it comes from the Latin *an*, meaning 'without' and *orexis*, meaning 'appetite'); whereas anorexia nervosa is a psychiatric term referring specifically to a collection of symptoms including an obsessive fear of gaining weight and critically limiting food intake. Clearly this book is all about my journey through anorexia nervosa. However, in popular language, this is almost always shortened to anorexia. That is why I have decided to use that term throughout. I realise that it would not be technically correct if this were a research report written for academics, but I believe that it is most helpful for this book written for the general reader.

Chapter One
I Couldn't Believe It

'She's not going anywhere. Her heart is struggling. She's not stable enough to move.'

I couldn't believe what the doctors were saying. I thought I was just going to the hospital for a check-up, and now they wanted to keep me in; not just in the hospital, but also in the bed, I wasn't even allowed to stand up or walk.

But then I couldn't believe much of what the doctors had said for many months. What was wrong with losing weight? That was how to be attractive, that was how to look good, how to be good. I thought the doctors had it wrong. I was fourteen years old, I knew my own mind, I could make my own decisions. Every few days, for months now, I had been in a doctor's surgery or clinic being weighed and measured, or in a consulting room being told about the dangers of what was happening in my body. And I simply couldn't believe them.

But now there was something different. My dad was there, even though he was supposed to be away in meetings, and he was looking worried. My mum, who had been firmly holding herself together for months, was very emotional. And the doctors, gathered in their huddle at the bottom of my bed, were talking about dangerously low levels of electrolytes in my blood, about cardiac arrhythmia (abnormal and irregular heartbeats) and the risk of cardiac arrest.

I had only agreed to mum taking me to the hospital because of the pain in my abdomen. It did hurt and I was scared. I'd put up with pain for many months, but this was much worse.

13

It began in my maths lesson. I liked maths. I loved quickly solving problems and working out solutions. But that day I couldn't concentrate. I couldn't think about anything other than the ache that had started in my lower back, and was spreading around the front, growing into an excruciating pain. By the time Mum picked me up, the agony was overwhelming. When we got home she tried to give me some water but I couldn't touch it.

When you are living with anorexia you experience overwhelming fears that make you see the worst in everyone and everything. As Mum offered me the glass of water a thought immediately rushed into my mind: 'She's stirred sugar into that, it's full of calories, don't touch it.' So, I didn't. At that time, the anorexia had such a control over my mind that I had hardly eaten or drunk anything for days. I couldn't even brush my teeth because of intrusive thoughts telling me that toothpaste has calories in it.

As I lay on the couch, Mum tried to get hold of Dad, but he was away in meetings with his phone turned off. So, she persuaded me that I should go to the hospital. I can't recall all the details of the admission, but now, as a doctor who has admitted patients, I can piece together the memories I have.

The doctor asked me endless questions about my life and health, about what had been going on recently and a detailed history of my eating pattern. The nurse came to record my vital signs; she took my pulse and blood pressure, and tried not to react at how dangerously low they both were. Then she tried to take my temperature, and this time she couldn't help but react. I vividly remember the look of shock on her face. She tried to take my temperature again, but to no avail. My body was shutting down so rapidly that my temperature was too low to be recorded.

Next, I was wired up to an electrocardiogram (ECG) to look for any changes in the trace of my heart. And blood was sent to the lab to check the levels of my electrolytes (including sodium, magnesium, potassium and phosphate). If a patient has had a highly restricted nutritional intake they are particularly at risk of low levels of electrolytes. This can have a devastating effect on the electrical activity of the heart, resulting in dangerous arrhythmias which can rapidly trigger a lethal cardiac arrest.

I can picture myself as the admitting doctor that day. I've been in similar situations in my daily job. These are the patients for whom your heart sinks. They are so unwell that you start to doubt that anything you do will make any difference, because their body is already shutting down. On that day, my body was shutting down.

I remember at one point telling them I needed to go to the toilet and a group of doctors watched me as I walked. I knew I was weak. I felt dizzy even when I had been lying down. Each step felt like I was walking in thick mud. I had to summon all my energy to continue moving forward, keeping my eyes open and focusing on what was in front of me. But I thought to myself, 'I'm walking, I'm OK, I'm fine.' Little did I know that this was the last occasion I would be allowed to walk for a long time.

Mum has written a diary every day for most of her life. Her entry for that night includes this:

Wednesday 22nd November 2006: Lizzie put on bed rest and taken to ward. Nick in London out of communication. Sending texts and phone calls everywhere telling people the situation. Feel desolate. Staying overnight with Lizzie, in a bed beside hers, but can hardly sleep. Eventually got hold of Nick. He will cancel meetings and be here as soon as possible.

I was scared, really scared. I didn't want to be in hospital. I would do anything I could to get out, except eat. I remember the nurses coming every two hours throughout the night to do their observations, taking my pulse, temperature and blood pressure. I remember people coming with food and saying encouraging things to me. I guess they thought they could tempt me to eat. But that was exactly how my mind interpreted it: a dangerous temptation that should be resisted.

I felt a bit better the next morning when Dad arrived, but still nothing could make me eat. The consultant came to see me, and then had a separate meeting with my parents. She made it clear that my body was in a dangerous state. If I didn't eat she would have to insert a feeding tube through my nose. But if I could eat then I would gradually be allowed out of bed, and eventually out of the hospital. Apparently, it was as simple as that! Nothing about what was happening in my mind, or what was causing me not to eat. Just a simple refeeding programme that would rebalance my electrolytes to a safe level, bring my pulse and temperature up to an acceptable figure, and thus render me safe for discharge – back to my world of anorexia.

When you live with anorexia you fight your own thoughts and fears, your own self, every second of every minute of every day. I knew that if I used all my focus and all my determination I could reach the targets this consultant was setting me. I also knew that it wouldn't make any difference to what was going on in my head, but it would get me out of the hospital.

So, when the next piece of food was put in front of me, I forced myself to eat it. Not because I wanted to get better, but because I was determined to get out of the hospital, and back to my ways of restricting food intake. Of course, the doctors now had to ensure that I didn't succumb to the other lethal condition known as 'refeeding syndrome', which may occur following a rapid intake of calories.

Normally, the body uses food to build stores of glycogen, fats and protein (this is known as an anabolic state). But, during starvation, the body switches to breaking down this store (known as a catabolic state). When nutritional intake is then suddenly increased the body switches back from the catabolic to the anabolic state. However, to start storing all of this new energy the body requires potassium, magnesium and phosphates, which are electrolytes that have been seriously depleted during the catabolic state. The resulting sudden and dramatic shifts in the body's fluid and electrolyte balance places the heart at risk of a dangerous arrhythmia, which could result in a cardiac arrest.

So, initially I was just given a quarter-portion of lunch, which I ate. Then a very small snack in the afternoon, followed by a quarter-portion of dinner, which I also ate. Over the days that followed these gradually became half-portions, then three-quarter and finally full portions.

I fought against my thoughts and fears in order to eat these meals, because I was determined to meet their targets and be released. I wanted to get out. I wasn't given any effective therapy in addressing those thoughts and fears that had brought me to this point. It was all about risk management as they tried to free up the hospital bed. At the time I didn't understand the pressures the doctors were under with bed spaces, nor the protocols they were expected to follow. And neither did my mum and dad, who were very concerned that, as they saw it, the emphasis was on getting me out rather than getting me better. In fact, at times, they became quite cross with the doctors because even though I was now actually in a hospital no-one was addressing the underlying causes, just the symptoms.

Over the many following hours that they sat by my bedside, Mum and Dad encouraged me to talk about my life. They helped me to reflect on what had led me to this point. We wrote down those thoughts in a journal (in fact, much of this chapter is taken from what we wrote together around my bed). This wasn't any formal counselling, or structured cognitive behavioural therapy, we just talked and wrote things down. But it did help me as I began to get some perspective on the preceding months. I told them things I had never shared before.

At that time I thought it had all begun the day I broke my leg. It was my brother Luke's birthday, 1st March 2005. As always we were having a family celebration but it also coincided with a scheduled horse-riding lesson. There was some question about whether I should go, but the course had been paid for and the family all decided that I should not miss it. I was the most reluctant, which was unusual because I absolutely loved horse riding.

I loved the smell of the horses as I approached the stables. I loved the sound the horses made when I got closer. I loved saddling up my ride and leading him out to the arena, particularly if it was set up for jumping – I loved jumping. It was my mum who usually took me riding, even though she didn't like anything about horses or what she described as 'smelly, noisy, dirty stables'. But she always took me faithfully to every lesson; even when she had literally just come out of a two-hour tooth extraction and her mouth was full of blood and dressings, still she took me and stood in the cold while I rode.

But this day, because Mum was doing a special meal for Luke, my dad took me. Perhaps my life may have been different if I hadn't gone, or Dad hadn't taken me, or at least if I had been concentrating fully on the jumping. My mind was half on the horse underneath me in the arena, and half on my brother waiting for me at home. A group of us at the stable were building up to some competitions so the jumps were quite high. As I approached the first one the horse must have sensed that my mind and body weren't totally focused. So, he refused. And because I wasn't fully concentrating I went over his head and landed hard on the ground, hurting my shoulder.

Dad's attitude to pain was always to 'tough it out'. Perhaps this came from the rugby fields at his school when Dad, who wasn't great at rugby and usually came off worse in a tackle, was taught to 'run it off' after getting hurt. He taught me the same. So, seeing him watching me from the side of the arena, I got straight back on the horse and tried again. If I wasn't focused enough before, I was certainly concentrating even less now. And the horse knew it. Again, he refused. This time he veered at the last moment and I fell straight off onto the jump, landing awkwardly on my leg.

I was in a lot of pain as I hobbled away, but I told people I was OK and someone kindly took the horse from me. Dad eased me into his car and drove me home. When we arrived, Mum had everything ready for Luke's special birthday meal, and I didn't want to spoil it. I was also quite embarrassed about falling off so stupidly. So, it was some time before I went to the hospital for an X-ray where they told me there was a fracture. Looking back on it now, I think it was probably a small greenstick fracture of the fibula, and possibly most of the pain was from the damaged ligaments in my knee. But, either way, the hospital decided that I should have a leg brace fitted and would be required to use two crutches for at least six weeks.

At the time I was attending an all-girls Roman Catholic school, and they had a rule that for health and safety reasons I couldn't attend while I was on two crutches because I would not be safe going up and down the stairs. Therefore, I was destined to spend that time out of school. I'd just turned thirteen and initially I quite enjoyed the prospect of sitting at home watching TV and reading magazines.

My mum and dad had recently started an educational charity which had a growing staff team, and they both needed to be at the office every day. So, every morning, Mum would help me gather everything I needed into a bag and take it down to the lounge. She, and Dad if he wasn't away, would come home several times during the day to spend whatever time they could with me. But hardly any of my classmates came to visit. I suppose they may have been jealous that I was having all this time off school. Each day I became increasingly lonely.

Mum had bought me craft to do, books to read and videos to watch, but I found the only thing that really consoled me was something else from Mum – her cakes and sweets. My mum is a great cook who makes fabulous food. I have always enjoyed it. Each day I would eat some homemade biscuits or fudge before heading off to the gym club, or swimming or dancing or horse-riding. Now I couldn't go anywhere, but I could still eat, and I did.

And the more I ate, the more I wanted to eat. The food comforted me, it made me feel better. I began to use food to control my emotions. I started to binge, eating until my stomach cried out in pain, and then just a few more mouthfuls. Mum and Dad didn't know how much I was consuming. But I knew. In fact, I became aware that it was getting out of control, and that I should stop.

As I lay on the couch, day after day, I spent a lot of time reading magazines and looking at the photos of beautiful celebrities. They were slim and so obviously attractive. Next to these pictures were articles about diets, and the connection was obvious. So I tried them. But they never worked. Mum's lovely food was always around and I couldn't resist it; I gave in to the temptation and ate another cake, another sweet, another biscuit. And then I felt such a failure. Where was my willpower? Where was my self-control?

Eventually, after physiotherapy, I was allowed to go down to one crutch, which meant I could return to school, and I was really looking forward to it. I hoped that I would fit straight back in with the other girls, and I wasn't prepared for the reaction I received. In the evening after my first day back I wrote in my diary, 'What have I done wrong? Everyone seems to hate me.'

I thought it must be something about all-girl schools, that we can tend to bring out the worst in one another, as we try to push ourselves up by pushing others down. Or perhaps it was the fact that I was always slightly on the outside anyway because I was serious about my Christian faith, as much as I understood it at that stage. Because, although it was a Catholic school, being serious about faith made people think you were slightly odd. Or perhaps it was just that the friendship groups had moved on, and the space where I used to fit had closed up.

Even the girl who had previously been my 'best friend' had changed. The school asked her to carry my bag for me, because although the school would let me back with one crutch, they wouldn't let me use the other hand to hold a bag. So, she was delegated to carry it. Except she didn't, she deliberately dragged it along the floor, making a big show of scraping it over the rough concrete. Mum had bought me that bag specially as a back-to-school present and it meant a lot to me. There was nothing I could do to stop this girl from ruining it. The more I asked her to stop, the more she scraped it.

But it wasn't just the general meanness that hurt me. It was the specific comments about weight that really got to me. I had put on weight, I knew it. I had been sat on a sofa for six weeks, eating too much food. I was an easy target for the other girls to pick on, as they made sarcastic comments and called me names. Nothing I did could make them stop.

I felt powerless. But Dad had always said that 'every problem is an opportunity' and I decided to take action. I decided to move schools. This time it would be a co-ed school, with boys as well as girls. I was convinced that boys would tone down the bitchiness of the girls.

My parents weren't so keen on the idea, but I had discovered over the years that if I put together a reasoned argument they would always listen and take it seriously. So, I began to research other schools that I could get to from our house by bus, train or bike, and that were co-ed.

Eventually, after a lot of discussion, we decided on a community school in Romsey, a train journey from our house in Southampton. It would mean quite a commitment to get up early, walk for half an hour into town and then catch the train, and walk again at the other end. But I was happy to do that, because it would take me to a new school, where I could start again, where there were boys as well as girls, and where they would accept me as I was.

I remember my first day at that new school as if it was yesterday. I was nervous and excited. Dad drove me there, prayed with me before we got out of the car and then walked with me to the reception. I was wearing my new blazer and white blouse. I felt smart, clean and ready to make a fresh start. The receptionist took me through into the school corridor as Dad walked back to his car. He told me later that he immediately phoned Mum to say 'I think she will be happy here.'

And I thought so too, as I was taken to a room full of pupils who would be my tutor group, the people with whom I would spend much of the next three years, the people who would be my friends. When I walked through the door all eyes were on me. The teacher smiled, welcomed me and invited me to find a seat.

As I made my way past the rows of desks one particular boy looked up and spoke to me. He was the first boy to say anything to me. In fact, he was the first pupil in the whole school to say anything to me. He looked me straight in the eye and said: 'Hello fatty'.

A Letter To Myself in Hospital

Dear Lizzie,

I know you are scared. You've suddenly been admitted to hospital and the doctors talk about the risk that your heart could stop. But take courage. You can get better. You can have a wonderful life, if you will fight the anorexia before it takes even more control.

I wish I could be you again. If only you could feel the pain I have experienced for the past ten years; every second of your life taken over by an internal bully. It hates you and wants to make every ounce of your existence miserable, and to make you hurt the people who love you the most. Tell me, is it worth it?

I don't have the chance to live those years again; I wish I did. But you do. Take the opportunity, run with recovery and don't give anorexia another glance. I wish I could re-write the last decade of my life. I can't, but you can.

Anorexia is a disease. It's not a diet. It will consume you. Right now, you don't want to lose it. You think it gives you control, but that's not true. Anorexia is a bully that is taking over your life. I know you sometimes like to call it 'Ana', as if it is a friend. It isn't. Please read this poem that I wrote some months after I was admitted to hospital, like you. And please think again:

My Friend Ana

My friend Ana
What sort of friend is she?
She tore me down completely
Took everything from me

My friend Ana
Is slowly killing me
Taking my enjoyment
My right to be free

My friend Ana
At least I thought she was
She stole my friends and family
And my life, just because . . .

I wanted to be perfect
To fit the flawless mould
Push down thoughts and feelings
And be thin until I'm old

The diets and the calories
Fill my thoughts throughout the day
My life is slowly fading
What more can I say?

My friend Ana
Her voice is bold and tough
But truth is: listen to her and . . .
You'll be dead before you're thin enough.

Love,

lizzie x

Chapter Two
Sticks and Stones

There's an old traditional saying that 'sticks and stones may break my bones, but words will never hurt me'. This saying may be old, and it may be traditional, but it's clearly not true. Because words do hurt. In fact, their impact can last way beyond the temporary break from a stick or a stone. They can set up thought patterns that go on to have a damaging ongoing impact on mental health. I know how destructive this can be, from my own experience.

I realise that the person who says damaging words often does not intend the consequence, and I certainly don't blame those who said things that affected me. They didn't do it deliberately. Anyone living with anorexia knows that acquaintances, friends or even family members can innocently say things that act as triggers of intrusive thoughts or fears, which contribute to the illness. Casually referring to a family friend as 'plump' can do this, because it triggers thoughts like, 'If they think she is plump, they must think I am massive'. And even the innocuous and well-meant comment, 'You are looking healthier' can trigger the thought, 'I must be putting on weight'.

I don't blame the boy at my new school who said, 'Hello fatty'. He would not have been aware of the impact that those two words would have on me. I am sure that he didn't really intend to hurt me. In fact, a few weeks later he asked me out on a date. (I declined politely).

I don't even blame the girls at my old school who were deliberately hostile to me. They probably had little insight into the impact their actions would have. Actually, when I appeared on *BBC Breakfast* a few years later, to be interviewed about the link between bullying and anorexia, some of those girls got in touch to say that they didn't realise the effect they were having on me.

But words and actions do alter a person's view of themselves, which can be significant in the development of an eating disorder. Research carried out by the national eating disorder charity Beat has shown that 86 per cent of people with eating disorders report that 'bullying', in its broadest sense, contributed to the onset of their illness, with 75 per cent reporting that this still affects them now. Those surveyed expressed comments such as: 'It caused low self-esteem which fuelled my eating disorder'; 'They called me names. They didn't count it as bullying as they were laughing, but it hurt'; and, 'The bullying had a control over me, and the logical reaction was to control my food intake'.

Of course, not everyone who experiences nasty things being said about them develops an eating disorder. Life is much more complex than that. When I was in the hospital, talking to my parents about what had brought me to this point, I told them I thought it began a few months earlier when I broke my leg, put on weight and nasty comments were made about my size. But as I thought more about it after that, I realised that there was something much more complex going on, with deeper roots. The seedbed of my anorexia was laid many years before that. Obviously, my particular story is unique to me, as is everyone's, but some principles are common to others who are living with anorexia, or at risk of it. And therefore, hearing my story, although it is personal, might help others in their own unique lives. So, let me take you back to my younger childhood, before we return to how I reacted when the boy said 'Hello fatty'.

I remember my years as a young girl being a very happy time. Good food played a large part. Mum was very careful about healthy eating; Saturday was our only 'sweetie day' when she put a small number of treats in two special bowls, one marked for me and one for my brother Luke. But she was also an amazing cook, so ordinary meals were extra-ordinary. As a family, we really enjoyed our mealtimes together. We would all sit at the breakfast bar, eating Mum's latest culinary delight, and talking about anything that interested any one of us. Everyone had a voice, and everyone was heard. Sometimes we would all try to speak at once, which led to some interesting experiences.

I vividly remember one evening when Mum said it would just be a quick meal of macaroni cheese. But no food was ever ordinary with Mum. She flavoured it with bacon and mustard, put it in a baking dish, covered it with a combination of cheeses and a sprinkling of nutmeg, then put it in the oven. Dad, Luke and I were gathered around the breakfast bar watching her, and all four of us were in an animated conversation, which continued as Mum took the meal out of the oven and placed it in front of us. The food was bubbling and sizzling, and so was our discussion. In fact, we were all talking at once, so Dad grabbed the plastic tomato ketchup bottle and banged it on the breakfast bar like a judge's gavel, saying, 'One at a time!' What he hadn't realised was that the lid wasn't on the bottle, and the most wonderful fountain of tomato ketchup showered us all. After an initial shocked silence, no-one was cross or upset, we all just laughed together.

Many people came to our house to enjoy the food and conversation. Our neighbours used to call it 'the party house' because they were always coming in for celebrations. Bonfire night was a big occasion each year, as Mum would create a huge cauldron of home-made soup, and a great variety of themed food. All the neighbours came, whatever their age. I remember an old lady several doors down who loved the food and the company but said she was too old to stand in the garden watching the fireworks afterwards. Not wanting her to miss out, Dad put a chair outside specially for her. Which was great, until one rocket went right up in the air and then came straight down on her head. Not exactly what Dad had intended.

Looking back on it now, what strikes me particularly about my childhood at home was the inclusiveness of my parents. Mum and Dad are Christians, but the people who came to our house were of all faiths and none. Even amongst our immediate neighbours we had atheists on one side, Muslims on the other, and Sikhs opposite. But they all felt welcome and valued.

This inclusiveness was also evident in a different way, when on Sundays my parents often put on special meals for people who were single. My dad used to say all were welcome, the only criteria was that you live on your own – and like roast dinners. It's not easy to cook a roast dinner for one, so for most of these people who lived alone this was the only time they had a home-cooked Sunday roast. And what a feast it was! Not just a roasted joint but also multiple types of vegetables, variants of potato, forms of stuffing, and loads of Mum's delicious gravy.

I loved those meals. It wasn't just the food; it was also the conversation. That was where I heard different ideas and viewpoints discussed and argued. Dad was always gentle with people, but rigorous with ideas. Luke, who went on to Oxford University and is now Head of Philosophy at a boarding school, says that those discussions around the dinner table were a good preparation for Oxford tutorials.

Mum and Dad were keen for me, and Luke, to be exposed to a wide range of views. They didn't see any harm in that. And I don't think there was. Certainly, my own personal faith developed as I heard many different beliefs being expressed and debated.

But, at the same time, Mum and Dad were very keen to protect me from any harm that others might do to me with their words. And, unwittingly, some of this prepared the ground for the thought patterns that led, in me, to the development of anorexia. I don't blame my parents for this at all. In the same way that other parents of people living with anorexia should not be blamed for any part they may have had in the process. My mum and dad certainly acted with the best of intentions. But they do say that if they had their time over again, they would do some things differently.

To understand how this developed, let me start at the day of my birth. On my left cheek I had a large cutaneous cavernous haemangioma. That's a type of malformation where a collection of dilated blood vessels form a benign tumour. Because of the trauma of birth, in my case with forceps, this presented as a large lump swelling out from my face. Dad says that when the doctor delivered me, she immediately took me over to the corner of the room where she kept me for some time, telling Dad to stay at the bedside. I have explained to him since that she would have been checking for complications such as impingement of the trachea or oesophagus, which could have affected my breathing or swallowing. But, in the emotion of the moment, Dad interpreted it as them keeping me from him. Certainly, before they handed me over to Mum and Dad, the doctor prepared them for seeing my face. And it was a shock to them. Dad has told me that he vividly remembers what he said to me as he took me from them and held me in his arms. He didn't say it out loud – I wouldn't have understood it anyway – but he said it clearly in his head, and in his mind he was making a definite promise to me. He said, 'I love you, my daughter, and I will protect you from whatever anyone else says about you.'

And that is what he did. It's what my mum did as well. From my earliest days, she made sure that I was always dressed in beautiful clothes, including special bonnets that covered the haemangioma. And if anyone made any comments about it, they were told 'it's a birthmark' and were met with a fearsome look from my parents that effectively ended that subject of conversation.

Thankfully, the swelling quickly reduced and the mark gradually faded, and could be covered by special make-up I got on prescription. All that is left now is some loose skin and what looks like a bruise, which can only be seen if I'm not wearing make-up. Most people don't notice it. Although, when I was working in the Accident and Emergency Department I wasn't surprised when a nurse asked if someone had punched me.

My parents' desire to protect me continued throughout my life. Mum and Dad did not want me to be upset or hurt in any way, whatever it cost them.

I remember when I was eleven years old, I had a friend for a sleepover at my house. My dad always wondered why they were called 'sleepovers' when no-one seemed to sleep. And, true to form, my friend and I were still awake at 2 a.m. My bedroom was on the ground floor of the chalet-bungalow in which we lived, and the path to the front door passed my window. There were street lights outside and so we saw a shadow on the curtains when a person walked up the path. A noise came from outside and so we tentatively opened my bedroom door to look. Through the large glass panel on the front door, we could see a person standing there. They were silent, and only moving to make shapes with their body and arms to scare us. We were petrified and screamed. Mum came running to us, and the person disappeared into the night. Dad was away lecturing at a college in Norway at the time, and Luke was off on a camp. We found out later that this night-time visitor was a very disturbed young man who knew our family, knew that Luke and Dad were away, and had deliberately come to scare us in the middle of the night. But, at the time Mum didn't know who he was or what he might do. She called the police, who said they could do nothing. So, she stayed up all night, in a chair outside my room, to protect me and my friend.

Mum and Dad couldn't bear the thought of me being hurt by other people and the things they said or did. But, of course, we live in a rough, tough world, and life hurts. They could not protect me from comments that people make, especially when those are innocently meant.

I was a very energetic child, keen to be involved in many activities. Gym was one of these. I loved the concept of using strength and agility to do dramatic things with nothing other than my own body. When the classes started preparing us for competitions, we were put into groups of three, to create routines and displays together. I was larger and stronger than the other two girls in my group and I vividly remember the teacher saying, 'You have a very stocky build, you'll be the base'. Consequently, I was always crouching or lying on the floor while the lighter girls struck graceful poses on top of me.

I don't know how many other people would find that this comment and resulting activity would be a trigger for them, but it was for me. I felt it as a criticism of my body, because I was sensitive about what other people thought of how I looked. I am sure the teacher didn't mean anything other than that this was the safest formation. But my mind perceived it differently.

In the same way, at ballet classes, in my mind I was the large one who wasn't graceful like the others. I loved the idea of ballet, I loved the music, the concept, the atmosphere. Every week I looked forward to being a part of the ballet community. But at the last minute, when it was time to drive to the ballet school, I would find every excuse not to go. Why? Because the room was lined with mirrors and I could see myself alongside the other girls who, in my mind anyway, were all much slimmer than me. They looked elegant, whereas I looked – what was it the gym teacher said? – stocky.

I simply wasn't prepared for people making comments about how I looked. And I wasn't prepared for people doing bad things to me. Yet, that is the way the world is. People criticise other people, and do bad things to other people. But I was sensitive to it from my birth. Of course, it's when you move from the security of your own family into the world of school that this becomes particularly evident.

I had the privilege of going to a lovely primary school. My mum was Chair of Governors, but that role was strategic, making decisions for the good of the whole school community. She shouldn't use it to advance me personally, and she couldn't protect me from the normal rough and tumble of life that the school experience brings.

It was at school where I discovered that people would steal the wonderful food my mum would so willingly share with anyone who came to our house. Each day Mum made me a special packed lunch. And it really was lovely. There were home-made biscuits and cakes in special wrappers with personal messages of love and encouragement that Mum had written on them for me. When we arrived at school, we all had to put our lunchboxes on a rack in the corridor. And from my seat in the classroom, looking into that corridor, every day I saw a girl from another class open up my lunchbox and steal my special food. I really didn't know how to cope with this. I never told the teacher, nor my mum (in fact, it was only when writing this book that I first told her about this), but I internalised a feeling of being picked upon. And it hurt.

When break time came, that feeling grew. Whatever we were playing, it always felt to me as if I was on the outside, never really accepted as part of the group. I remember some of us often used to play a game where we had an imaginary home with an imaginary family that acted out scenarios. The roles changed each day as the other girls jostled for position, to get the best parts. But I stood back and, eventually, when I asked what part I could play, they would say: 'You can be the maid in the corner doing the washing-up.' I was always the maid, every time; I never got to be the princess. I didn't know how to push for position, how to ensure my inclusion. I'd been brought up in a home where everyone was included and all were welcomed on equal terms. And so, when I was not included at school, I felt rejected. And it hurt.

But it was probably birthday parties that had their greatest effect upon me. My parents used to arrange the most amazing parties for me and my brother. They were huge productions, and were sometimes themed around a popular TV show of the time. For example, in 2003, when I was eleven years old, the first series of *I'm a Celebrity Get Me Out of Here* had recently been a big hit on TV. So, my parents put on a version for my party. In the morning, various members of my class came to our house for my mum to film them recreating legendary scenes from the show. One played the role of Tony Blackburn, obsessively collecting logs. Another acted the part of Rhona Cameron delivering to camera her famous speech, popularly known as her 'sometimes' rant. Each had a part and all played them brilliantly. Through the afternoon my dad edited all the footage to make short video features like on the show. And then in the evening, everyone gathered for a live event, with challenges and bushtucker trials, interspersed with the video features, which we watched on a screen. It was a great party and we all loved it.

But what was most important to me was that everyone was invited and included, not just a select few. That was what my parents believed was right, and that was what I assumed was right – to be as inclusive as possible. So, when it came to other people's parties I was deeply hurt when I was not invited. I didn't understand that they probably had limits on the number of people who could attend, and they had to make difficult choices. I felt rejected. And it hurt.

Thus, in those early years of my life, I started to develop what is known in psychiatry as 'overvalued ideas'. My beliefs were reasonable, they were not delusional (it was true that I wasn't being included in those parties), but they were pre-occupying me to the extent of dominating my life. My beliefs about my own value and worth started to revolve around the idea that I was being excluded, and I had to change in order to be accepted. This began to cause me an excessive amount of distress.

Running in parallel with all of this was another aspect of my personality that I had also derived from my parents. I worked hard and set myself high standards. I wanted to make my life count for other people, to make a difference in the world. When I dreamed at night, it wasn't about fairies, it was about fighting, and I always had to win. So, when I studied at school, I wanted to achieve the highest possible marks. But no matter how hard I tried, I couldn't. Neither I, nor my parents, knew at the time that I was dyslexic. My mum had suspected it because she also is dyslexic and recognised some of the symptoms that I was exhibiting. Therefore, she asked the school to arrange for a dyslexia test.

I've had two dyslexia tests in my life. One was then, at primary school, and the other was many years later, at medical school. The test at medical school was a proper one carried out by an expert. It took three hours and included an IQ test. I remember this experienced examiner saying that she was surprised by the result. She discovered that I was in the bottom 1 per cent for dyslexia, but the top 1 per cent for IQ. She wondered how I had got through education, let alone got to medical school. And she said that I had clearly been able to develop my own strategies for coping with the dyslexia, but unfortunately had missed out on so much support that is available for people who are diagnosed earlier. The test at primary school was very different. It was carried out by a teaching assistant, and all I remember of it was her poking me in the back with a pencil while I stood with my eyes closed. It only lasted a few minutes before she declared that I did not have dyslexia, I was sent back to the class, and that was the end of that.

As a result, I struggled at school, even though I worked as hard as I could. And to me it seemed like a lot of attention was given to the top students, who were destined to achieve great things, and a lot of attention was given to those at the bottom, who were provided with extra support. Even though I worked very hard, I was in the middle. And, because I knew I ought to do much better, I felt rejected and worthless.

So, there I was. A young girl with high ideals and a thwarted desire to achieve, with overvalued ideas about rejection and exclusion, and a negative body image.

Now, as a doctor looking at even that brief summary of my case history, there are evidently clear risk factors for anorexia. But at the time I couldn't know that. All I knew was that I felt deeply hurt by the actions of the girls after I had put on weight when I had broken my leg, and I felt crushed by the comment of the boy on my first day at the new school. In themselves these were not big events. But, given my predisposition, they were powerful. And they set me on a course towards the anorexia that consumed my life for the next ten years, and almost took that life altogether.

A Letter To Myself as an Eleven Year Old

Dear Lizzie,

I know you don't think this now, but people are not intentionally trying to hurt you, they are not deliberately trying to leave you out. They are just behaving as most people do - trying to push themselves up by pushing others down. That's the way the world is.

Please don't think that you will only be accepted by other people if you change yourself. Take joy in who you are. People come in all sorts of different shapes and sizes. There isn't one ideal mould that we all must fit. All of our different lumps and bumps make us unique in our own special way.

Striving to be the one who is slim and slender won't bring you happiness; it won't make you feel loved or included. Actually, it will do the opposite, as you will start to hate yourself. Trust me, that internal bully in your head is much more painful than an external one in the playground.

But also, don't be afraid of getting upset. It's by hurting that we grow. It's OK to be sad about not being invited to a party. It's OK to cry. It's OK to feel hurt. After all, life hurts.

Love,

Lizzie x

Chapter Three
So Quickly

I don't know how I got through the rest of my first day at my new school. I was devastated when that boy said 'Hello fatty', and in my mind I immediately assumed that everyone else thought the same. Therefore, I must be really fat, too fat for anyone to like me or be my friend. I was desperate to be accepted and included. So, I had an automatic response to start a very strict diet.

That wasn't easy, because I loved food. Those who have not lived with anorexia often assume that those who do must hate food. Why else would they not eat it? That is not true. I have always loved food; I love how it tastes, I love how it smells, I love the feeling of comfort that comes from a full stomach.

But I was now driven by an overwhelming need to lose weight, even though that meant the pain of hunger. People living with anorexia experience constant pain. It's not just the hunger, it's also the pain of being constantly cold, of aching muscles and exhaustion. But I had to cope with that physical pain because the emotional and psychological pain of failing to lose weight was far greater.

There are many risk factors for anorexia. Some of these are more potent than others and some are contingent and cumulative – that is, they only come into play in the presence of other factors and they build upon them. For me, one of these was my ability to cope with pain.

Perhaps it came from my parents. My mum has osteoarthritis, which means that she lives with a constant arthritic pain in her knees and hands. Sometimes it is so bad that even holding a pen to write, or a spoon to cook, can be agony for her. But it doesn't hold her back; she pushes through and carries on with her life. Similarly, my dad has always viewed pain as something to ignore and 'run off'. When he had a very full diary speaking at universities across the country he would never let people down, no matter how ill he was. He once did a whole week of speaking engagements while he had pleurisy (an inflammation of the lining of the lungs which can be very painful).

Whether I inherited it or learned it, I don't know, but I wouldn't let pain or illness stop me. I remember one winter, when I was ten years old, I had been ill for weeks and felt fatigued every day. But I kept going. I got up and went to school, and then on to my activities every evening. Every day was a battle, but I wasn't going to let myself give in. Even when my illness was diagnosed as glandular fever, I wasn't going to let it stop me. That New Year, when my dad was fulfilling one of his regular lecturing responsibilities in Norway, he had the opportunity to take the family. I wouldn't let my glandular fever stop us all from going with him.

Coping with pain is a positive trait. But, like many other positive traits, when combined with anorexia it can turn in on itself and become negative. This is what happened to me.

There I was, at my new school, desperate to be accepted, and I started to restrict my food intake, ignoring the pain. Dieting became 'my friend'. Almost all of the other pupils in my year had been together since Year Seven, and I came in as the 'new girl' in Year Nine. On reflection, I think they really tried to include me but I had such a strong overvalued belief about being excluded that I often sat on my own, thinking about dieting, working out how I was going to avoid eating that day so that I could lose more weight.

I remember that an ice cream van used to come to the school each break time, and most of my classmates got a tub or a cone. But I didn't. I always found an excuse why I couldn't eat one with them. I overcame the hunger pangs and resisted the temptation. And that made me feel like I was in control. No-one and no thing, not even my own body, could make me eat. I was going to lose weight and then, I thought, I would be accepted and included.

My mum was still making me her wonderful packed lunches. But when I got to school, I often gave them to my classmates. They got to enjoy my mum's wonderful cooking, and they certainly ate well! In my mind, I derived a perverse pleasure from seeing them eat my food as I thought, 'This will make them put on weight, not me.'

In the evenings, I started to take over some of the cooking from Mum. That's another feature of people living with anorexia: we love to cook food. My mum rarely uses other people's recipes; her knowledge and experience enables her to create her own. And I followed that example. Except, whereas Mum was motivated to make the food as healthy and tasty as possible, I was driven by the irresistible need to make it as calorific as possible. So, I put in as much butter and cream and fat as I could.

Again, if you are not used to anorexia this may sound very strange. Why would someone with anorexia make such fattening food? It's because I knew I would not eat it but my family would. And in my mind, if I could make the rest of my family eat more calories and fat than me, then I might feel better about the minimal food I allowed myself to eat.

Over the course of my illness I learned many strategies to avoid eating the food, but I am not going to explain them all here for obvious reasons. At that time, what I did was simple: I 'ate' on my own. My family knew that I wanted to be a doctor, and therefore I had to study very hard. So, instead of us all eating together around the breakfast bar as we had always done, Mum and Dad let me put my food on a tray and take it to my room to eat while I studied. I did work while I was in my room, in fact, I studied very hard. But I didn't eat the food.

It was at this time that I also took up running. I loved it because I felt I could run away from everything that was happening in my life: the fact that I wasn't happy at my new school, the fact that I hated my body. I could run away from all of it. And it also burned calories.

Like restricting my food, running made me feel in control.

Our house was right by the university campus, which is on the edge of Southampton Common, a huge area of trees and grass and lakes and paths. Each morning I would run all over it, around and around until my body hurt so much I felt like I was about to die. And then I ran some more. I couldn't bear the thought of spending the rest of the day feeling guilty because I hadn't run to the absolute limit, I hadn't burned those extra calories.

I had to get up really early to do this, because I knew I must get back before the family sat down to eat at 7 a.m. in order to do something before breakfast began. For as long as I could remember, Mum had always laid out the food the night before, each of our bowls filled with our favourite cereals, and covered with clingfilm. So, I had to get back in time to empty almost all of the bowl, so that when Mum came to the table I could appear to be just finishing my last mouthfuls.

Of course, running makes you hungry, and the pain from my empty stomach, combined with the pain in my legs, gave me a perverse pleasure. I could conquer the pain. And I was getting thinner.

In fact, I was losing weight so fast that none of my clothes fitted me anymore. So, Mum suggested a special mother-and-daughter activity to go out clothes shopping, followed by a nice meal. For once, I enjoyed trying on clothes. The most stylish and figure-hugging outfits now actually fitted me. I remember particularly finding a tartan skirt with a matching tartan corset. It was different, it felt unique and special. I tried it on, and it fitted me. And for a brief moment, as I looked in the dressing room mirror, I actually liked what I saw. Looking back on it now, I think, at that point, I was probably at a healthy weight. And if I had been able to overcome the drive to restrict my food, if I had eaten appropriately, and run sensibly, I might have had a healthy body.

But I didn't. I couldn't stop restricting my food intake. It had become like an addictive drug. After the happiness of shopping for clothes with my mum, the meal turned into a battleground. What should have been a lovely end to our special time together turned into a dreadful row, as I tried every way I could to avoid eating the dinner.

People living with anorexia often use tricks and techniques to make it look to others like they are eating, when they really are not. One of these can be a sign of the development of anorexia. When eating with others, I, like many others in the early stages of anorexia, began to cut my food into very small pieces. I would then move it around the plate to make it look as if I was eating, when I really wasn't. That is what I did that night. But Mum noticed and tried to make me eat the dinner properly. I wouldn't. I couldn't. The intrusive thoughts in my mind about not eating were just too powerful.

I don't know at what point my life had changed from me controlling my eating to my eating controlling me. But it had certainly happened by then, just three months after I had started at my new school.

So quickly.

Anorexia can take hold of a person's mind with frightening speed, without them really being aware of it, or even recognising it. That is why it is so important for family and friends to know the most common early signs and symptoms so that action can be taken before the disease progresses. This illness develops very quickly, and early intervention really is important.

By now, Christmas was approaching. And for the first time in my life I was dreading it. Christmas, when so much of the celebrations focus around food, is a very difficult time for someone with an eating disorder. In our house my parents followed the church calendar, in which Christmas is not just one day, but a season of twelve days known as Christmastide. And that is preceded by the season of Advent. So, on the first day of Advent my dad would put up the special Advent calendar. This wasn't the usual cardboard box with synthetic chocolate. It was a large felt construction with pockets for each day. In each of these Mum would put special chocolates. And in several of them (we never knew which), behind the chocolates was a folded up piece of paper on which Mum had written a riddle for us to solve. This told us where we would find a small wrapped-up Advent present (usually something practical that we needed anyway, such as a jumper, pyjamas or slippers, but the fact that it was wrapped up and hidden made it feel special).

I had always loved this, and looked forward to Advent each year with eager anticipation. But not this year. The thought of having chocolate to eat each morning filled my mind with panic and dread. While Dad fixed up the calendar I took Mum aside and tried, in every way I could, to persuade her that this year I wanted carrot sticks instead of chocolate. Once again, it turned into a row.

The combination of this row and the one after the shopping trip, in both of which I had been beside myself with anxiety and anger, convinced my mum that something was seriously wrong with me. She tried to share her concerns with my dad, and I vividly remember that night, sitting at the top of the stairs, listening to my parents arguing downstairs. Mum was trying to explain to Dad that I had developed anorexia. But Dad was having none of it. He kept saying that Mum was overreacting, that there wasn't really a problem, that it was just a phase and it would soon pass.

I remember being revolted that my mum had even said the word 'anorexia' when talking about me. How could I have anorexia? I'd seen pictures of people with that disease, and they were like skeletons. How wrong I was. People of all shapes and sizes can have an eating disorder, and it is a common misunderstanding that to have anorexia you must be very thin. This is simply not true. The reason some newspapers and magazines publish pictures of people who have become skeletal is because of the shock value, and that appeals to a certain type of reader who will then buy their publication. This is deeply unhelpful.

I thought it was not possible for me to have anorexia because, in my mind, I was so fat. When people live with anorexia they often develop a form of 'body dysmorphia', which is a delusional belief that one's body is severely imperfect. When this occurs within a case of anorexia the person often has a delusional belief that they are larger than they are. I did.

But, perhaps unconsciously, my mind also took note of the fact that Dad did not realise that I was restricting my food. So, I saw him as someone I could easily deceive and manipulate. He could be my ally in the battle against my mum. From then on, my distorted mind that was driving me to restrict my food, also did everything it could to drive my parents apart, to set one against the other, to divide and conquer.

When anorexia strikes, it affects the whole family, not just the individual person. All families are different, and respond in different ways. However, there are common reactions to anorexia across a wide variety of families, and it can be very helpful for parents particularly to know that it's not just them who feel like this.

That night, after the argument, Mum went outside and got into her car. She told me later that she had sat there for hours on her own, crying. She cried out in pain. She cried out in despair. She cried out to God for help. There's an old saying that goes, 'Faith isn't faith until it is all that you are holding onto'. And looking back now, I am so glad that she held onto her faith – her faith that God still had me in his hands and would somehow bring good out of this bad situation.

Meanwhile, Dad waited inside the house. He still didn't believe that I had developed anorexia, but he was concerned about how he had upset Mum. He was confused and conflicted.

Mum and Dad have always had a very close relationship. They were childhood sweethearts, in fact, Dad was Mum's House Captain at Junior School, but they only met properly when Mum was fourteen. A relationship developed and they got engaged when Mum was seventeen, and married when she was nineteen. Throughout their long relationship, right from the very first date, every evening they have always gone for a long walk to talk together (except for the years when Luke and I were too young to be left alone in the house). Even when they were working together in Canada for a year and it was minus forty degrees, still they went out every night, to walk and talk together (much to the surprise of the locals who often stopped their cars to ask if this couple walking through the deep snow were in trouble). Mum and Dad said that walking together was one of the best ways to enable talking together, and they encourage every couple to do this, particularly when they are going through tough times.

No matter how different their views were about what was going on in my head and in my body, Mum and Dad kept talking to each other about it. That is why they really embraced the family therapy, which started a few months later. But, it would be eleven long months before Dad finally accepted the seriousness of my illness, eleven months in which Mum felt she was fighting Dad's reluctance to recognise the situation, at the same time as she was fighting the anorexia which made me determined to lose weight. However, through it all, they walked and talked every day, and they stuck together, and held the family together. I am truly thankful that they did.

Christmas came and went. It was a very sad occasion, as I hardly ate any of the wonderful special food that Mum had prepared. The new term started at school, and still I continued to lose weight. I also started to develop some good friends in my class. I realise now that this would have happened anyway as I settled in, but, in my mind, I associated gaining friends with losing weight. So I continued to be driven by a compulsion to restrict my food intake and to exercise excessively.

It is hard for people to understand how that compulsion feels. But sometimes it's helpful for them to look at it in the context of other disorders that often occur alongside it – what, in medicine, we call comorbidities.

Obsessive-compulsive disorder (OCD) often accompanies anorexia. It is the presence of obsessions and compulsions, either individually or combined. Obsessions are unwanted, intrusive thoughts that the person often knows are ridiculous. Compulsions are repetitive behaviours that a person feels they have to complete for fear of the imagined consequences if they don't. So, for instance in my case, I became obsessed with the fear that our house would catch fire, all my family would be killed, and it would all be my fault. Consequently, every night I went through a repetitive series of checking the plugs. I would start with the plug socket behind my desk. I put my finger to the switch to check it was off, and I would do this again and again until I had done it exactly one hundred times. And then I would do the same with the plug beside it. Gradually I'd move around the room. If anything interrupted this routine, I would have to go right back to the beginning and start all over again.

Self-harm is another comorbidity that often accompanies anorexia, and certainly did in my case. This is the act of causing yourself deliberate pain as a mechanism to cope with difficult emotions, thoughts, feelings or situations. Physiologically the pain creates a release of endorphins that make you feel better, but that is only part of the drive to self-harm; there is much more going on psychologically, particularly in the context of anorexia. It is to do with self-hatred. If you hate the way you look, and you hate the way you still keep putting food in your mouth (no matter how small that amount may be), then a tension builds up inside, and you think it will only be released by self-harm. And when you do self-harm, the release of endorphins makes you feel better, which reinforces that behaviour in the future.

As the months went by, and winter turned to spring, the paths through which I ran each morning must have become bright and beautiful, but my world was becoming increasingly dark and ugly. All I could think about was losing weight and doing exercise. And home life had become a constant battle with my mum. I was continually lying to her, and she knew it. She could see through my tricks for avoiding food, and she challenged me about them. How I wish I had simply cried out to her for help, rather than shouting back in anger. But I couldn't. The compulsion to restrict my food intake was too strong. The fear of gaining weight was too powerful. The hatred of myself was too overwhelming.

Mum really didn't know where to turn. Looking back on it now, with the benefit of hindsight, she realises that she should have taken me to the doctor straight after Christmas. But Mum is from a generation and a culture where you don't want to bother the doctor, especially about something that doesn't seem obviously medical. However, research evidence shows that early intervention is really important with eating disorders; it has a major impact on recovery, particularly preventing them from becoming chronic.

Thankfully, I was a girl and so there was one change that Mum thought was sufficiently medical to enable her to take me to the doctor. By May, I hadn't had a period for four months. Technically known as amenorrhoea (an absence of periods for at least three cycles), this occurs in anorexia as a result of low body fat, which alters the secretion of hormones, including those needed to continue the menstrual cycle.

In my own heightened state of anxiety, my lack of periods worried me for another reason. I was petrified that I was pregnant. Of course, that wasn't possible. I was fourteen years old and had never had a boyfriend. In fact, I had never even kissed a boy let alone done anything more. But that's the nature of mental health, where one fear sparks off another, so one descends into a spiral of anxieties. Actually, that is no different from physical health, where one illness can lead to another. For example, it's not unusual for patients, after being admitted to hospital for an acute illness, to develop a chest infection or urinary tract infection, which needs further treatment, which then has additional side effects, placing them at risk of developing a further illness. And so it is with mental health, one condition can lead to another comorbidity, and another, which is again why early intervention and proper treatment of the underlying issues is so important.

On Tuesday 23rd May 2006, because I was anxious about my lack of periods, I agreed to go to the doctor with my mum. As I recognised earlier in this book, every person's story is unique and all will have different journeys up to and beyond this point. But what is consistent across everyone who develops anorexia is that all will have that first visit to the doctor.

It can be a really positive experience or a negative one. It can be a crucial turning point, or just another staging post in the continual harm that anorexia does. Which of these it is depends upon the knowledge of the doctor, and the willingness of the patient. Unfortunately, in my situation, neither of these were present.

I was totally unprepared for what would happen. I thought we were just going to talk about my periods, but Mum had other ideas. She told the doctor about my restriction of food intake and extreme exercise. Now, one might assume that since the GP is the first port of call for anyone with an eating disorder, they would know how to spot the signs and symptoms, would understand the sensitivity of that particular point in the person's journey through the illness, and would know exactly what to say and do. Unfortunately, for me, that was not the case.

My story is not unusual in this aspect. Many doctors do not know enough about eating disorders because they don't feature very highly in medical training, as I was to discover when I went to medical school. We had just two hours on the subject throughout the five years of study. And since many students didn't see it as core to their training, only half of them turned up for it.

My GP clearly had very little knowledge of the subject. She was insensitive, making unhelpful comments, and asking inappropriate questions. This was not a positive experience. So, my mum asked the doctor specifically to make a referral to the Child and Adolescent Mental Health Service (CAMHS). Thankfully, the doctor agreed to do this and my mum was relieved.

We stood up to go, and just as I was walking through the door, the doctor called me back for one final question. 'Do you make yourself sick?' she asked. Until that point I'd not thought about that way of losing weight, but now the idea had been suggested to me, by a doctor, I couldn't get the notion out of my mind.

A Letter To Myself After the Family Row

Dear Lizzie,

What a wonderful day out with your mum, if only you could see how lovely you looked in those clothes. I know you almost caught a glimpse of it today. But then you felt you had to push that thought out of your head. You couldn't bear to have a positive view of yourself.

Can you see that your mind is making you look at yourself as if in a distorted mirror? Where others see a lovely young girl, you can only see fat. But it isn't there, not really. And even if it was, it wouldn't matter, because you are who you are. You don't have to fit an image. Just be yourself.

Deep down, you know that your mum loves you whatever you are like. And so does your dad and the rest of your family. And so do your true friends. Can you find a way to love yourself?

I know it upsets you to hear your parents arguing about what is happening to you. And you know that this will only get worse if you keep trying to push them apart. But it's not really you who is doing that, not the real you. It is the disease of anorexia that is taking over your mind.

You can push back against it. Instead of fighting your parents, you can fight the disease.

It's not too late. You can turn your life around right now. But you have to take control and decide to work with your parents instead of against them.

It's up to you.
Love,

Lizzie x

Chapter Four
Conflict and Trust

2006 was meant to be a summer of celebration. For the family, it was to include a once-in-a-lifetime holiday to America, before my brother Luke went up to Oxford. For my future, it was to herald the start of my GCSEs, which would be the first set of exams on the long road to fulfilling my dream of becoming a doctor. And, for my faith, it was to mark a significant step as I would be baptised and confirmed. However, anorexia changed all of this. The family holiday was cancelled because no-one would cover me with travel insurance; my future as a doctor looked increasingly unlikely as I spent less than ten weeks in school throughout that year; and my faith, which should have provided a foundation of inner comfort and strength, became a source of personal conflict and struggle.

My parents had been saving for years to take us as a family on a special road trip across America. Several of Dad's books had been published in the USA, and he had been there a number of times as a speaker, so he wanted to share the country with us all. Mum had bought the air tickets long in advance so she got the cheapest prices, and as a family we were preparing the detailed itinerary. However, this was soon to be yet another casualty of my developing disease.

When Mum and I had left the doctor's surgery on 23rd May neither of us knew that the referral to CAMHS would come through so quickly. It was just over two weeks later that Mum took me to my first appointment at their Brookvale clinic. She was pleased that at last there were knowledgeable people with whom she could talk about what had been happening to me. However, I remember looking at her, the person I trusted so deeply, and feeling dreadfully conflicted because I was, in that moment, experiencing an overwhelming hatred for her. Why was she turning on me like this? Why was she exposing my secrets? Why was she collaborating with people who were obviously going to try to stop me from losing weight?

This conflict in my mind continued when I was taken off to another room to talk with a psychiatric nurse, on my own. She asked me if I believed that people cared about me. Thinking of my family, I replied, 'Of course they do, but I don't particularly care about myself.' Then, indicating the clinic in which we were sat, she continued, 'Do you think we care about you?'

I understood from that question, and her implicit reference to the whole of Brookvale, that she was communicating that she cared about me, and so would others at the clinic. I was deeply conflicted. How could they care about me if they wanted to stop me from losing weight? Getting thinner was good, it was how to be accepted by other people. If they cared about me, why would they want to stop me doing something that was so important to me?

For a moment I had a brief insight, one of a number that would occur over the months and years that followed as I progressed in my journey through anorexia. Perhaps here were people I could trust, people who cared about me and could help me find a different attitude to my body and the food I put in it. And certainly, looking back on it later, that is what they were. The people at Brookvale were not just highly trained and experienced professionals, they were also real people with a genuine humanity and compassion. I have carried that experience through into my training to be a doctor where, as I learnt the necessary facts and skills, I also sought to retain my humanity and develop my compassion.

But, at that moment, on my first visit to Brookvale, this insight set up a conflict in my mind. Here were people who cared, but they were also people who would try to make me eat. And such was the power of anorexia, I was immediately determined to fight back against them.

Dr Suyog Dhakras was the consultant at the clinic who was in charge of my care, and with whom I developed a love-hate relationship. I loved his humanity, I loved his honesty, I particularly loved his laugh. When I argued with him about the calories in a handful of nuts or a pot of yoghurt, he would laugh. He wasn't laughing at me, but nor was he laughing with the 'me' that was refusing to comply, because I was deadly serious and determined. I felt that he was laughing with the 'real me' who was still there inside, despite the ravages of the anorexia. He was encouraging that pre-anorexia me to gain insight and to realise how bizarre my life had become, where I would argue with such aggression about why I shouldn't have to eat that handful of nuts or pot of yoghurt.

Alongside the humour and the humanity, Suyog used a combination of rewards to encourage me into eating, and consequences to keep me safe when I refused. One of these concerned the forthcoming holiday to America. My parents, for whom truth and integrity is crucial, had contacted their insurers to check that our travel insurance would still cover me, given my current condition. The insurers said that they could only cover me if we had a letter from my doctor saying that I was fit to travel. Suyog was concerned about my safety and challenged me to battle back against the anorexia by putting on at least two kilograms in the next two weeks. Now I realise that it wasn't my actual weight that was important, it was the fact of eating properly in that period to stabilise my system, and I can indeed see this as entirely reasonable. But at the time my mind could not accept it. I could not put on weight, I could not overcome my fear of eating, even if it meant that the family holiday had to be cancelled.

Those who have never lived with anorexia may find it hard to understand how I could do this to my family. And unless you have experienced it on the inside, perhaps it simply isn't possible to understand the complex internal conflicts that develop in the mind as the anorexia increasingly takes hold. You might, quite understandably, think that I was trying to get 'my way', as if I thought

I deserved what I wanted, and as if I thought that my desire to lose weight was more important than the rest of the family's desire to have this holiday. In fact, in the complexity of my conflicted mind, quite the opposite was going on. By that stage I didn't think I deserved anything. I didn't think that I deserved to eat. I didn't even think that I deserved to be comfortable. That was why I increasingly slept on the floor, rather than in my bed. I didn't think that someone as awful as me should have the comfort of a bed. And certainly, as my weight continued to drop, and more bones protruded, sleeping became increasingly painful – just what I thought I deserved. I loved my family and didn't want to hurt them, but I hated myself even more than I loved them, and I couldn't eat that small amount that was needed to reach the target for us to go on that holiday.

So, my parents had to cancel the flights and stop the plans. Mum did discover that the insurance rules were different if we stayed in Europe, and she used the money that was left to book a holiday in a cheap hotel in Kos. She tried to enable us to have a special time together. It was good being a family on holiday on this Greek island but, of course, the anorexia came with us.

It was there that I found that I could continue to deceive my dad in my constant drive to lose weight. Dad and I had always loved special father-and-daughter activities. Throughout my childhood he had endeavoured to find different and exciting ways in which we could head off somewhere together. And we did the same on Kos; we hired bikes and cycled over the island.

Dad really didn't have a clue about calories or my schemes to lose weight. So, he would happily cycle long distances with me, as I counted the calories that I was burning. And when it came to lunch, he would innocently agree to my order of a large green salad, with the dressing 'on the side', which I conveniently left. When we got back to the hotel Dad would tell Mum that I had eaten a good meal, whereas in fact, it contained hardly any calories at all.

By the time we returned to the UK I had lost even more weight and I was becoming progressively weakened. It was at that time that

Brookvale began to provide us with family therapy. Initially all four of us went: Mum, Dad, me and Luke. But when Luke went up to Oxford he could no longer join in, and I always resisted the opportunity to engage because I was so worried that these sessions would expose more of the tricks that I was using to avoid eating food.

However, Mum and Dad found the therapy immensely helpful, even when Luke was gone and I was not engaging. And I will always be grateful for what the therapists did in helping my family – even though I certainly didn't show it at the time. Reflecting back on this now, I realise what a thankless task it is for so many professionals working in mental health. As a hospital doctor, I find that almost all the patients and their families are immensely grateful for what the medical staff do. Those working in mental health do not always experience that same appreciation, and we need to find some way to acknowledge and reward them appropriately.

As the days passed, the holidays ended and the autumn term began at school. I entered Year Ten, the start of my GCSE years, and I had my sights set firmly on being a doctor. I knew that it would be a challenge to get into medical school, but I was up for it. In fact, I would do anything it took to make the grades. Anything, that is, except eat. Here again I faced another conflict. I wanted to achieve at school, but I couldn't overcome the intrusive thoughts about restricting my food intake. And this was putting me in serious danger.

My life now was a constant round of appointments with the nurse at the GP's surgery to monitor my health and take regular blood tests, and meetings with Suyog at Brookvale to make decisions about what I was safe to do. I always argued with him about this, and the weight targets that he set for the next meeting, and the meal plans that would be necessary to achieve them. He always responded with that laugh of his, in a firm but encouraging way. The meetings were supposed to end with an agreement, but I often refused to sign it.

The staff at Brookvale were amazing. I remember one psychiatric social worker who used to drive to my school in Romsey and pick me up to bring me back to Southampton for appointments at the

Brookvale clinic. And on those car journeys we would talk. Once again, here was a genuine person, with a real humanity, not just a professional doing a job.

The GP's surgery, however, was a whole different story. The doctor told me that there was nothing wrong with me, except that I wouldn't eat, and she was surprised that I was allowed to go to school at all, given my weight. But it was the nurse whose lack of knowledge and understanding really compromised what Brookvale was seeking to achieve, and even put my life in danger.

Each week the nurse would weigh me and take my blood pressure. Now, anorexia is a very deceptive illness. It turns you into a liar and a cheat. The nurse, apparently, had no knowledge of this and was easily deceived. She always weighed me in the clothes I was wearing, and it was very easy to manipulate the reading and achieve whatever target was set for me that week.

But the real risk came from her approach to reading my blood pressure. She wanted to be able to enter a reading that would be acceptable. On one occasion, as I had become increasingly malnourished, my blood pressure was particularly low. She should have recorded it and escalated the issue immediately, calling the doctor to assess me. But instead she told me that she couldn't enter such a low figure and needed me to bring up my blood pressure to an acceptable level. So, she told me to run up and down the stairs so that it would give her the figure she needed. At the time, I was specifically barred from doing any exercise, and following her instructions put me at risk of a potentially dangerous collapse. But, such was the control that anorexia had on me, I relished the opportunity to burn up some more calories and I ran up and down as many times as I could.

Of course, there were limits to how much I could manipulate the figures at the weigh-ins. And often Suyog told my mum that it was too dangerous for me to go to school the following week, so I must stay at home. You might think that this, of all things, would be a wake-up call that would make me fight back against the anorexia.

I had been told that it was vital that I got good GCSEs as well as A Levels if I was to get to medical school. And that was one target on which I was really set. But such was the hold that anorexia had on me by that stage, even being told that I couldn't go to school did not overcome the fears I had about eating, and the obsession with losing even more weight.

A major step in my life happened to coincide with the development of anorexia. In the spring of 2006 I decided that I wanted to get confirmed. My mum and dad were attending the local parish church, and had been for many years. But when I was born they went to a non-conformist church, which meant that I was dedicated rather than baptised. Therefore, before I could be confirmed in the Anglican Church I had to be baptised. Our vicar suggested baptising me in the sea at Calshot, together with a few friends who were in the same situation. That baptismal day, 20th May 2006, was a very special time for me, as was my confirmation the following morning, which was carried out by the Bishop of Southampton (now Bishop of Durham). I remember praying something like, 'God, whatever I go through I want to trust you, and know that you love me.' But making a commitment like that in your mind is not the same as knowing it in your heart and living it out in your life. This was one stage in my spiritual journey, it wasn't the destination.

On the day of my baptism, my Grandparents (mum's parents) gave me a lovely pocket Bible, with a pink cover. I still use it today. And inside, my Grandpa had handwritten the words of Proverbs, chapter 3, verses 5 and 6: 'Trust in the Lord with all your heart and lean not on your own understanding; in all your ways acknowledge him, and he will make your paths straight.'

This is now a really important Bible passage for me. In fact, I say it over to myself each day when I walk to the hospital, as I pray that, whatever I face in the day ahead, I will trust God. At the time of my baptism I really wanted to do that. I wanted to trust God with all my heart. But my heart was also home to the dreadful illness of anorexia, which was causing me to lie and cheat, and to damage my body. And so, what should have provided a foundation of inner comfort and strength, became a source of personal conflict and struggle.

It was just two days after I had been confirmed that my mum had taken me to the doctors, and just over two weeks later that I had started at Brookvale. Every day, as I fought against Suyog and my parents, I also cried out to God to help me to trust him. But I kept on restricting my food intake until I became so ill that, six months later, I was suddenly admitted to hospital.

A Letter To Myself After Confirmation

Dear Lizzie,

What a wonderful weekend you had for your baptism and confirmation. And what a significant step this was for you on your own personal spiritual journey.

I know that you were really touched by the Bible verses your grandad gave you. But I know that this has also set up a conflict in your mind. How can you trust in anyone when you won't let go of the control you hold? Why has the trust you used to share in your family become replaced by conflict? And why can't you trust the professionals, when you know they care about you?

These are questions with which you will have to wrestle as you continue your journey. But know this: there is a hope and a future that is available for you. When I was in your situation I wrote a poem called 'Trapped'. It was bleak and hopeless. But now I'm further on in my journey I have changed it, and renamed it 'Walk'. I've kept the first two verses from the original, but added a third since then.

Have faith, it is possible to start trusting again.

Walk

I'm trapped inside my thoughts
Consumed by all my fears
The world outside is moving
They never see my tears

Days are quickly passing
And I just sit and pray
My happiness is fading
Inside I'm dull and grey

And yet the sunrise promises
A brighter, better day
Over the horizon
If I can walk that way

Love,

dizzie x

Chapter Five
What's the Answer?

When the consultant told me that I could be released from hospital if I ate the food, and achieved a certain weight target, I forced myself to do it. Initially it was quarter-portions, then halves, then full meals. I managed to eat because I was driven by a desire to get out of hospital, away from the doctors who were controlling my life, and back to being able to continue my own food restriction regime. That motivation to get back to my old ways enabled me to overcome my drive not to eat. But it was also a – very brief – moment of insight for me: it was possible for me to overcome my thoughts and fears about eating.

If there had been some effective therapy at this point, perhaps I may have been able to recognise that this same determination could be applied to ridding myself of anorexia altogether. But that wasn't available, and I continued to spiral deeper into this dreadful disease.

Reflecting on this now, as a doctor, I am aware of the difference between the way the hospital responded to my admission, for what was fundamentally a mental health issue, and the way that we respond to those we admit for an issue with their physical health. For example, if we have a patient come in with pneumonia, we treat the symptoms, but that is only the beginning. Yes, we might give them some paracetamol for their fever or some codeine for their pain. We might give them some oxygen and, if they are having difficulty breathing, we might use some saline or salbutamol nebulisers to open up their airways. But the most important part of our management would be prompt provision of adequate antibiotics. We know that it is not enough just to treat the symptoms, we must also treat the underlying infection – the fundamental cause.

Looking back over all of my interactions with health professionals, as I received both community and hospital care for anorexia, it is plainly obvious that symptomatic management accounted for the vast majority of the expenditure of time and resources. And this clearly was not the answer. The focus on weight gain and an increase in oral intake, without effective application to addressing the underlying cause, was equivalent to treating someone with pneumonia by focusing on paracetamol, codeine, oxygen and nebulisers, but without giving them any effective antibiotics.

Of course, I know that there is no simple treatment for anorexia. Since I have journeyed through this illness, and qualified as a doctor, many have asked me the obvious question: 'What's the answer to anorexia?' That is even a question that has been posed to me by experts in the field, which shows how little is really understood about the disease. The response I give, from my experience, is that there was no one comprehensive turning point for me. Sadly, there is no magic bullet to cure anorexia. There is no tablet that can be taken, nor injection that can be given. But that doesn't mean that there is no answer. The unhelpful word in the question 'What's the answer to anorexia?' is not the word 'answer', it is the word 'the'. Anorexia can be beaten, if we invest sufficient resources in helping people to address the damaging thought patterns, no matter how difficult and complex that may be.

What is clear is that education and early intervention are particularly important. Appropriate education of people and their families will help them to identify potential risk factors and to spot the signs and symptoms at the initial stages of the development of an eating disorder. Then, appropriate early intervention to address the underlying issues is necessary in order to prevent the eating disorder from continuing to develop.

But once an eating disorder has really taken hold of the person's mind, as anorexia did in my case, then what are the steps towards recovery from that stage? To my knowledge, and in my experience, the key is that the person must take back control and learn to use their determination to fight the disease, rather than fighting against the professionals and family members who are seeking to help them. Only they can do this. No-one can force them, and imposing a weight-gain regime can be counter-productive. Each individual is different, but the process of regaining control and applying their determination in a positive direction might involve gaining some insight into the reasons for their particular thought patterns (as, for example in my case, I have described in chapter two of this book). But, it certainly will involve gaining insight into how they can change their thought patterns as they move forward with their lives. This will take time. It is not a quick, easy process. In the same way that the journey into an eating disorder takes place over time, through multiple damaging occurrences, so the journey through it will take time, over multiple insightful occurrences.

What happened in my journey was that there were lots of little epiphanies, brief moments where I gained insight into the fact that I could fight back and regain control of my life. Of course, my experience is individual, it isn't definitive, but I hope that there are principles that can be derived from it which will help others. Indeed, that is why I am writing this book.

The realisation, in that hospital bed, that I could force myself to eat was a moment of insight. It was a small one, and it only made a marginal impact on my journey at that point. But it was one staging post along the way. A much greater one, which had a much bigger impact, was to come a few weeks later. But before I tell you about that, let me explain the events that led up to it.

As with most hospital patients, I was only allowed visitors at specific times. My mum and dad came in at every possible opportunity. They sat by my bedside. They talked with me, they played games with me. Often they brought letters from other members of the extended family. My grandma, who I loved very much, wrote to me almost every day. But I never opened her letters.

I couldn't bring myself to read them. I hated myself so much that I couldn't bear the thought of reading her words in which I knew she would tell me that she loved me. How could anyone love me when I was such an unlovely person?

As the days passed, my brother's first term at Oxford came to an end. Mum and Dad drove him back to Southampton. On the first day home from the first term at university, most students go out with their old school friends to celebrate together. But Luke didn't do that. Instead, he came straight to the hospital to see me. I can vividly picture that Saturday evening as Luke, Mum and Dad sat around my bed watching *The X Factor* on a tiny portable TV.

I guess that others looking at us would think, 'What a happy, peaceful family'. We were anything but. One of the debilitating features of many mental illnesses, is that the person who is experiencing it, and their family, tends to feel isolated and alone. They feel that they are a failure, living in a world of successes. They look at other people, and other families, and they see them as happy and peaceful, enjoying life in a way that they never could. But the reality is that everyone suffers, because life hurts for all of us – individuals and our families. The night before I had been taken into hospital I had gone with my mum and dad to see the new James Bond film, *Casino Royale*. From the outside we probably looked like a family without a care in the world. But on the inside, that was not at all how we felt.

This is why I believe it is really important that we are all open about the struggles we face. Then, perhaps, the stigma of mental illness will begin to melt away. And maybe we will be able to face the reality together, as a common humanity. According to Mind, the mental health charity, one in four people in the UK will experience some form of mental health problem each year. And since most families contain more than four people, that means most families will face it with them.

As I reflect on my journey through anorexia, I am so pleased that my family stayed with me and did everything that they could in order to help me. It could not have been easy for them, not least because one of the worst aspects of anorexia is the way in which it leads people to deceive those who are closest to them, and that they love the most.

One of the reasons I wanted to get out of hospital was so that I could try to get back to my deceptive programme of exercise. In the weeks leading up to my admission, Suyog had specifically banned me from any exertion. But I had found ways around it: I could still exercise to burn calories, and I could hide this from my parents. Unable to go out running, I had discovered that there were parts of the house where I could exercise without being spotted. The only computers in the house at that time were in the converted garage, which was my parents' office at home (what I used to call 'The Home Office'). This has a concrete floor, so when I told my mum I needed to use a computer, I could go there and do star jumps without her knowing. I would record the number in my diary and set myself a target every day. Once she did notice the strange figures alongside my journal and she asked me what they were. I lied. I told her that this was part of my therapy – to record the number of bad, intrusive thoughts I experienced each day. I even tried to persuade her that it showed how well I was engaging with CAMHS.

Mum had also discovered the evidence of my other exercise spot, a corner of my bedroom where I did repeated press-ups and sit-ups in the night. Mum noticed that the carpet was getting worn in a strange pattern and challenged me about it. I lied again as I tried to cover up what I was doing. I don't recall exactly what story I made up in my attempt to get out of this discovery, and nor does Mum, but I do recall that she was not convinced.

Despite this, Mum showed me the utmost love at all times. No matter how badly I was treating her, still she clung on to her faith that what she called the 'pre-anorexia me' was still inside there somewhere.

Because it was the season of Advent when I was in hospital, Mum wanted me to have some form of Advent calendar. She didn't want to repeat the debacle of the previous year's chocolate calendar so she found another solution: a jewellery calendar with a different ring, or item to go on a bracelet, for each day. They were each put in little gossamer bags and I loved opening them every day, during the evening visiting hours.

Mum has told me since how every evening, as she drove to see me, her heart broke that little bit more. With Christmas approaching, her route to the hospital took her past houses in which people were turning on their fairy lights, and going out to parties. And here was her daughter, cooped up in the hospital, with her life closing in around her, in a prison of anorexia, unable to enjoy the wonderful world outside.

Dad showed his love in a different way. He always carried a Bible in his jacket pocket and, as he sat on the bed, he would ask me if I wanted to read some of it with him and to pray. I always said yes, and one of those readings was another little insight for me. Dad read from John's Gospel (chapter 10) in which Jesus said, 'The thief comes only to steal and kill and destroy; I have come that they may have life, and have it to the full.' I recall, after he read that verse, how he stopped and read it again, slowly and thoughtfully. We talked about it for quite a while and I remember it dawning on me that anorexia was like a thief, stealing my happiness and killing my joy. That night I wrote in my diary: 'I must stop, otherwise the thief will destroy my life. This is not fair. God and my family love me and that's all that matters.'

Of course, that was not the end of my anorexia, but it was another staging post in my journey. Despite this realisation that God and my family loved me, I still struggled to even consider letting go of the anorexia. It was still my best friend. It was always there with me, and I still firmly believed that if I could satisfy that eating disorder by reducing my food intake and increasing my exercise, then I could be loved.

The days passed, and on 7th December, two weeks after I was admitted, the consultant concluded that I was fit to be discharged, although apparently still not safe enough to walk, so my dad had to push me out in a wheelchair, and put me in the car. The sun had just gone down and, in the gathering dark, Mum decided to drive on a little detour. There was a large housing estate near our home, with many families who seemed determined to outshine one another each year with their Christmas light displays. Mum drove us round and round the estate. The lights were gaudy and tacky, but I loved them.

As we drove, Mum reminded me of how, the weekend before my admission, we had gone to see the Southampton City Centre Christmas lights turned on by the Australian TV soap actor-turned-singer, Craig McLachlan. He was appearing in the show *White Christmas* at the Mayflower Theatre and Mum told me that she had managed to get seats for 29th December. If I met whatever targets Suyog would set for me before then, perhaps he would deem me well enough to go with the rest of the family. I was really excited about this. I didn't know then that nine months later Craig would become the source of yet another insight on my journey, for much would happen over that time. Indeed, much happened over the next two weeks.

Having been discharged from the hospital, I was back in the care of CAMHS, and back to the weekly meetings with Suyog. Once again I would argue with him about meal plans and weight targets. I remember most of one session being taken up with a discussion about the fact that I had refused to eat a slice of chocolate cake. I argued, as vehemently as I could, that this was OK because I had eaten some strawberries instead. It may be hard to understand such an argument. It seems ridiculous and laughable. And of course, in his warm human way, Suyog did laugh. But when anorexia has such a control over your mind, these tiny things assume mammoth proportions. I could not, and I would not, eat such a piece of cake. And I would argue, with all the energy I could muster, that strawberries were equivalent.

But a bigger battle was looming on the horizon. My mum's birthday would be on December 20th. For many years, we would always celebrate by going out for a meal as a family. But, at this time, I was not allowed to leave the house. Mum did not want me to be excluded, so she planned to have a takeaway delivered instead, and she told me that it would be Chinese food. The thought horrified me, and led to another long dispute with Suyog who set, as another target, the challenge of eating a plateful of this Chinese takeaway. I refused it, and sat through my mum's birthday celebration without eating anything. In fact, I refused all of my food that day. This caused a dreadful row with Mum, who did everything she could to make me eat. This should have been her special day, but I would not budge, I could not.

I am so thankful that Mum is such a warm and forgiving person because not only did I ruin her birthday, I then did something even worse. To this day I don't really know why I did it, except that I was in so much pain and I wanted her to be in that pain with me. In a strange way I thought that this might bring us closer together. When Mum wasn't watching, I went to the kitchen drawer and got out a large pair of very sharp scissors. I took them up to my mum and dad's bedroom and, overcome with immense hurt, anger and pain, I aggressively cut the bedsheets into shreds, on my mother's side.

When Mum discovered it, she dissolved into tears. The bed was her safe space, her sanctuary. This was where, at the end of the day, she would sit to read the Bible before lying down to close her eyes and dream of a world without anorexia. And I had violated it.

But even worse was to come, with the same pair of scissors. Since my admission to hospital, my dad had definitely changed his attitude to my restriction of food. Before this I had seen him as my ally. He was easy to deceive when I didn't eat and, even when I did, he had no idea about calorific values or fat content. So, when Mum objected to me eating just a salad, I could get him on my side to argue against her. But now, he backed her up at every point.

The morning after Mum's birthday, she had put out in the kitchen one biscuit and one mini chocolate muffin for me to eat. Exasperated and exhausted by the events of the previous day, she asked Dad to make sure that I ate them. When I saw the plate, I became very angry. Why had she included a mini chocolate muffin? Why not just two biscuits? I tried to persuade Dad that I should not eat the muffin. But he stood firm, insisting that this is what was on the plate, as per Suyog's meal plan, and therefore I must eat it.

I argued back and became furious that Dad would not budge. I tried to get out of the kitchen, away from the food. But Dad would not move from the doorway. I tried to push past, but in my weakened state I was no match for him, as he just stood there blocking the way. And so, in my desperation and anger, I went back to the same drawer as I had the previous day, got out the same large pair of very sharp scissors, and held them like a dagger as I lunged towards my father's chest.

He stood still, with both arms stretched out, across the doorway. He didn't move. He didn't try to defend himself. He just stood there, looking at me.

The human brain can work at amazing speeds, and mine must have done so that morning. Because in that split second, as I was lunging the scissors towards my dad, I had another powerful moment of insight. How could I do this? Did the anorexia have such a hold over my mind that I would even risk stabbing my own father? At that moment, I took control, and I stopped myself, with the blades inches away from my dad's chest. That was me, the real me. I took control. I stopped myself. For that moment, I had power over the anorexia.

Now, if this was a fictional story written by a screenwriter for a film, perhaps this would be the final climactic resolution. I would drop the scissors and fall into my father's arms. My mother would join us for a tearful family hug as the demon of anorexia had been exorcised. The final scene would probably show us happily sitting together eating another Chinese takeaway.

But real life is not like that. This was not the end. There was much more that I, and my family, would face. It was, however, one of the most crucial staging posts for me in my journey through anorexia. No matter how powerful was the drive in my mind not to eat, I knew that I could take control of it. Anorexia could be beaten.

A Letter To Myself After I Took Control

Dear Lizzie,

Today you turned a potential tragedy into a triumph. You stopped yourself from doing something terrible, and you realised that you can take control over anorexia.

You have already learned the most important lesson that will enable you to overcome this dreadful disease. The key is in your hands. You can fight back against that bully in your mind. You can defeat it.

I know you feel too weak to do this. But today you discovered how your love overcame your anger and fear. Love does that. It is powerful. I know you find it hard to love yourself, and cannot believe that you are loved. But you are.

I wrote the following poem when I was in your situation. I hope it will speak to you.

Please Save Me

I'm bound by all my fears
Locked away in pain
I can't stop her voice
I give in once again

I'm holding on
With one last thought
Begging for mercy
It's my last resort

Alone in my room
I quietly plea
For someone out there
To rescue me

Love

dizzie x

Chapter Six
PEGs and Pressure

For as long as I can remember, I have always loved musical theatre. I love the stories, the lights, the costumes, and most especially, the songs. There is something in the music and lyrics that stirs the soul in the depth of my heart. And so, on the night I was discharged from hospital, when Mum told me that she had got tickets for *White Christmas*, I really wanted to be there.

The subject was raised at a meeting with Suyog and he set me a steep target to show that I was well enough to be out at such an event. After all, it was only a few weeks since I had not even been allowed off my hospital bed. But I was determined to achieve it. And I knew I could; I had taken control in order to eat enough to get out of hospital, and I had taken control to stop myself from stabbing my dad. I could do this.

And I did. I managed to just about meet the target. So, we went down as a family group, with my grandparents who had come to stay for Christmas. Mum had somehow managed to get tickets right at the front and I loved being so close that I could see into the eyes of the actors. Craig McLachlan didn't know me from Adam (well, Eve anyway), but I felt that I had some kind of connection with him because I had watched him turn on the lights just before I was suddenly admitted to hospital. Now, here I was, a few feet away from him and the other performers. I was back out in this wonderful world, with all of its opportunities and enjoyments. I was no longer trapped in the prison where anorexia had held me.

However, in the interval, something switched in my mind. Suyog had said that not only must I achieve a weight target to get to the theatre, I also had to eat an ice cream while I was there. And, as the curtain fell at the end of the first act, it felt as if the prison bars of anorexia came down with it. I was immediately overtaken by intrusive thoughts about not eating. After all, we were already here. I could now refuse to eat. What would Mum do then? March the whole family out of the theatre? Well, yes, actually she would. And Dad agreed. Much to the horror of my grandparents, Mum and Dad both made it absolutely clear that if I would not eat an ice cream, then we would all leave.

Suddenly it seemed that I was no longer in control. And the only way that I could wrestle back the power would be for me to dig my heels in and refuse to eat. But I didn't want us to miss the second half. So, I negotiated and argued all the way through the interval. As the concessions were just about to close, and people were coming back from the bars to take their seats, Mum and Dad said this was my last chance. Either we got an ice cream or we left. At the very last moment I agreed to a frozen yoghurt. Even in that decision, the anorexia was back in control, determining what I could do: because a frozen yoghurt cannot be eaten quickly, it would take time, and somehow I would find a way of ditching it. But Mum and Dad, who were sat either side of me, were increasingly wise to my tricks. The whole of the second act was punctuated by them letting me know that they were watching my every move, and if I tried to avoid eating any of the yoghurt, we were all going to leave.

Once again, the anorexia had turned an enjoyable event into a battle. But more than that, it had turned me back within myself. I lost the sense that I could beat anorexia. Deep in my heart, I wanted to be free of it. I wanted to be out in the world that I was experiencing that night. But this would never happen through targets and meal plans.

I cannot fault the dedication and commitment of the CAMHS team. By now they had started a new regime to try to force me to eat. Every meal time, three times a day, one of the team came to our house and sat with us as we ate, and then for another hour afterwards, accompanying me to the toilet to ensure that I didn't vomit it up.

Mum and Dad found this very difficult. For Dad, who has always seen meals as a time to talk and discuss issues, he felt awkward that joining us at the table was someone who wasn't there for the conversation, but just to make sure that I ate. For Mum, who still needed to work full-time with Dad in the charity they had co-founded, this meant that she had to structure her day to make sure that all the meals were ready exactly on time. In fact, I only discovered much later how much of a pressure my illness had put on Mum and Dad's working life. The charity began to experience financial difficulties and the trustees started applying pressure for them to lay off staff. But Mum and Dad wouldn't do that. These were people with families and mortgages, and my parents didn't want our family problems to be the cause of their family's distress. So, Mum and Dad just worked harder, very late into the night and very early in the morning.

This was probably the darkest time for my parents. Thanks to supportive friends, who would come and sit with me some evenings to make sure that I didn't exercise, Mum and Dad went out for a walk as many times as they could, to talk together. But their conversations became increasingly depressed. They talked about how they felt that they were in a dark tunnel, so long and dark that they couldn't see any light at the end. In fact, they even came to fear that there never would be any light at all, that this wasn't actually a tunnel but a cave, and they were just going deeper and deeper into the darkness.

The people at CAMHS began to get concerned about them, for they knew that if my mum and dad became burned out then this would make my illness even worse. So, they arranged some temporary respite care through the local Behavioural Resource Service (BRS) who agreed to have me in their centre each day for a couple of weeks. I didn't want to go, of course, but yet again I didn't have any choice. It was agreed that initially I should try it out for a couple of hours. So, on Saturday 27th January 2007, a cold, wet day, they dropped me off at 9 a.m. and then went out for coffee at a local hotel, before picking me up again at 11 a.m. They said that those couple of hours felt like a taste of heaven as they could get off the rollercoaster and relax for once.

I was supposed to eat a snack at BRS, but I refused. And the staff didn't know how to handle this. They were obviously used to dealing with young people who had all sorts of behavioural difficulties, but they had no idea about someone living with anorexia. I subsequently spent two weeks going there each day, and found it very easy to get rid of food, and to do exercise, because they never monitored me going to the toilet.

Once again, I was losing a lot of weight, and Suyog began to talk about the possibility of a residential inpatient hospital in Winchester, called Leigh House. Now I know more about the provision of mental health services across the country, I am conscious of how immensely fortunate I was. Many people must wait a dreadfully long time to access inpatient services, and even when they do, they may then have to travel hundreds of miles away from home. Remember, I had my first appointment at CAMHS just two weeks after being referred by the GP, and their clinic was only a few minutes from our home. Now, I was to be referred to a residential inpatient hospital that was only ten miles away, and it was only a matter of days between Suyog first mentioning it and me going for the initial assessment.

But, speed of access and closeness of provision is not all that is required for effective treatment. As I was soon to discover, Leigh House was a mixed blessing.

It was on Monday 19th February that Mum drove me to that hospital to meet with some of the staff. Leigh House is a very modern building set in the countryside, with its own grounds in which rabbits live wild and run about everywhere. You enter through a security gate and park the car by a grass roundabout, which I later discovered also served as the location for a ritual lap of honour on the leaving day of any patient. There was more security to pass through the front doors and then you were in. It was a low-level purpose-built construction, a cross between a budget hotel and a hospital.

That day, Mum and I met with a number of the staff team and what struck me, very powerfully, was that they talked about therapy to address the underlying issues. At last, here was a place that would help me to get better. It was not just a place to prevent me from dying, and then discharge me back to my old life; it was not just a place to impose meal plans and weight targets. This was a place where I could get well again, and get on with my life once more.

That night, Mum wrote in her diary: 'Lizzie very upbeat and says she wants to go there.' And I was. And I did. That was where I wanted to be. I had just turned fifteen years old and had never really been away from home, but I felt so trapped in the world of anorexia, I desperately wanted to be free, I wanted to get well and to restart my life.

Mum and Dad were also very keen that I should be admitted. This wasn't because they were tired and felt unable to cope any more. Yes, they were exhausted, but they would do anything to help me, no matter what it cost them. They were keen for the same reason that I was. Here was a place that offered professionally delivered CBT to deal with the thought patterns through which anorexia held me in its grip.

Dad, in particular, was delighted to see that the therapy at Leigh House was provided by a clinical psychologist. He knew something about this profession because he, himself, had a degree in psychology. Dad often said that he wished he had paid more attention to the clinical aspect of the course (what, in his day, was rather pejoratively called 'abnormal behaviour'), but he had skipped most of those lectures because his interest was in cognitive psychology, particularly the relationship between psychology and computer science in the new emerging field of artificial intelligence. But when he went on to register for a PhD in this field he had friends who were taking up post-graduate study in clinical psychology. He knew that this was a competitive course, and even once they had secured a place, they would study to Masters, even Doctorate, level before taking up a clinical job. So, Leigh House offered therapy at the highest possible level. And that is what one would expect, because an inpatient unit was the 'end of the line' for treatment of anorexia. There was nowhere else to go beyond that.

Therefore, a week later, as Mum drove me through the security gates, I told her that I wanted to stay until I got well. Despite the growing knot of anxiety and fear in my empty stomach, I had a hopeful expectation that this was a place in which I could overcome anorexia.

I was put through an admission process, which included measuring my weight. Here at Leigh House they knew many of the tricks and techniques used by people living with anorexia, and so they got a true weight reading. This caused considerable concern, and the medical team talked about taking me immediately to a general hospital where I would be fed by a tube through my nose. This immediately evoked a conflict in my mind. Amongst people living with anorexia, being tube-fed is almost a badge of honour. It's a sign that you could resist food enough to have reached that level. However, it also means relinquishing control over what you eat. I wanted to be in control and I wanted to get better.

The medical team told me that I had until the end of the day to eat a quarter-portion or I would have to submit to a tube. So, I was assigned to the Positive Eating Group (called PEGs for short), made up of about a dozen people, all roughly my age. There were other young people in Leigh House, for a range of mental health issues, and we mixed together to watch TV or play games in the communal room. But, as I was soon to discover, that was rather limited. Because a large part of my days would be spent with the PEGs, in the dining hall.

Very shortly after I arrived, before I had even unpacked into my room, it was time for evening dinner. I was taken into the dining hall where I sat at a large table with all the other PEGs. This was the first time I had ever been with anyone else who was living with anorexia, and here I was about to face food with a group of them. It was very traumatic. In front of each of us was a carefully prepared and portion-controlled plate of food. And the fear was evident on the faces of the PEGs around me. We were all expected to eat together, watched very closely by at least three staff, and no-one would be allowed to leave the table until we had all eaten and drunk everything, every single crumb. I eventually finished my quarter-portion five and a half hours later, and was then sent to bed.

The inpatient strategy was based upon peer pressure. No-one wanted to eat, but no-one wanted to be stuck in the dining room either. So, those PEGs who had taken a bite of their meal would pressure others to do the same. 'I've done it, now you have to' was a common phrase around the table.

Anorexia affects a person's mind in many ways. One of these is to magnify their competitive nature. Amongst the PEGs, no-one wanted to be the first to eat or, worse still, the first to finish. Everyone wanted to be the last. So, as if in some surreal 'Mexican standoff', we would often sit there for hours looking at the food and refusing to touch it. Sometimes, this would mean that one snack or meal would run into the next, at which point, without us leaving the table, the plates would be cleared away and replaced by a number of build-up drinks of equivalent calories, as well as the next snack or meal. On some days, we never got out of the dining room at all.

We might not have eaten, but we did talk. And that is where I learned a whole new set of tricks and techniques to hide food. Looking back on it now, some of them were really bizarre behaviours. We learned to do all sorts of strange things to make it look as if we had eaten the food put in front of us.

The same applied to exercise. When we had reached a certain weight and calorific input we were allowed to use the hospital gym, and we certainly did make the most of every second we were there. But apart from the highly controlled gym sessions and weekly swimming, the PEGs were specifically banned from doing anything to deliberately burn calories. Of course, we found ways around this. When we were released from the dining room, after we had all cleared our plates (not necessarily into our stomachs), we found locations in the grounds where we were out of sight of anyone except the rabbits. There we would exercise vigorously for as long as we could.

At night, the nurses would check on us to ensure that we were asleep in bed, and not exercising. That was really easy to circumvent. Not long into my admission I had developed a reputation with the staff as someone who could be very persistent with trying to burn calories. There had been complaints from the other PEGs about noises in the night. All fingers pointed to me and I got put on hourly checks to ensure I was asleep, and to monitor my pulse to see if I had been exercising. But their reliability was their own downfall. I knew when they would be coming and so, in-between these visits, all though the night, I marched up and down the corridor and did star jumps in my room. It wasn't until a nurse suddenly came up between the hourly checks that I finally got caught.

The day after I had been admitted, my mum and dad were allowed to visit and eat with me. I sat on a table with them, instead of being with the other PEGs. They were shocked at the change in my behaviour in just twenty-four hours. My attitude to food had clearly deteriorated. They said that the way I looked, the way I sat, the way I touched the food, all demonstrated how I had quickly adopted the institutionalised behaviour.

And where was the therapy that we had all expected? Well, we discovered that there was a rule that none of the PEGs could have this until they had reached a certain target weight. Mum and Dad were told that there was no point in me having therapy until I reached that weight because my cognitive functioning was impaired by the lack of nutrition, and therefore I would not be able to engage with it. But they weren't buying that. As far as they could see, my brain was working as well as it always had done. And certainly, it was functioning well enough for me to learn all the new tricks and techniques from the others. However, rules were rules, and the CBT was not available for me.

I was able to take part in some art therapy, when I wasn't stuck in the dining hall. We were encouraged to write and draw and paint to express our feelings. That is where I developed my love of writing poetry, and some of the poems in this book were written in Leigh House. It is also where I found that drawing and painting could be highly cathartic as I was able to express visually what I could not describe with words. This was helpful, and I am thankful for it.

I am also thankful for the friendships I developed with the other PEGs. Like prisoners in a jail, we bonded together, united against the common enemy of the staff who tried to make us eat, but also in a largely unspoken way, united in our underlying desire to beat this disease and get on with our lives. My parents came in as often as they were allowed and I remember Dad reflecting on the dreadful waste of life that he could see in the group. Here were young people with so much potential that was bottled up in this building. I felt the same. There was so much that I wanted to do with my life, but I couldn't do it there, I couldn't do it while my whole mind focused around avoiding food. I had to get better and get on with my life.

Days turned into weeks, and weeks turned into months of the same routine, much of it spent sat around the table in the dining hall. When my parents visited, I was allowed to go out of the security gates, over the road into the fields, where the only possible walking route took us to a cemetery, which was morbidly ironic. Occasionally we had some wonderful treats as the staff took us on day trips to the seaside. They were very special, as we got a glimpse again of the world outside. We were also allowed to study, even though apparently we weren't at a suitable weight for our brains to function enough to engage with CBT. I actually took one GCSE while in the unit.

Sometimes, when a PEG had reached their target weight, we had a celebration as they were discharged, and we all waved them off. We would stand as a group outside the front door, waving and cheering as they drove round the grass roundabout on their lap of honour. But, as they then went through the security gates, we would be ushered back inside, back to the table in the dining hall. And, tragically, for some of them, it wouldn't be long before they were driven back through those gates for another admission.

I won't tell you how I learned to cheat the system, but I found a way in which I could appear to be putting on more weight than I was. Thus, I was apparently up to the target where I could receive the CBT. And that was transformational.

My therapist was a clinical psychologist who only came in for a limited time each week, but part of that was now spent with me. She was wonderfully skilled in her profession, and she had a warmth and humanity about her, treating me as a real person with my own beliefs and values, rather than just a professional project.

CBT is a form of talking therapy which helps people to manage their mental health issues by changing the way they think and behave. It is based on the concept that our thoughts, feelings and actions are interconnected, and that negative thoughts can trap us in a vicious cycle. CBT aims to help by breaking down issues into smaller parts and enabling people to change negative thought patterns. Unlike some other talking therapies, CBT deals with a person's current problems, rather than focusing on issues from their past. It looks for practical ways to improve the person's state of mind on a daily basis.

Through this therapy I began to think differently about what was important in my life. And, most of all, I began to see how my faith in God could change my perception of myself, and the world around me. For too long I had been focused on food and weight, as if that was all that life was about, but now I began to gain insight into the fact that, in God's eyes, those issues were tiny compared to the opportunities to live for him and make a difference in the world. I began to see that if God loved me whatever I was like, then what would it matter whether other people liked me or not. Gradually, I even began to learn how I might be able to love myself again. I began to change my focus from the weight I could lose in my body to the good I could do in the world. I began to regain a positive vision for my life. And I recognised that I could not achieve anything of any value if I kept starving myself.

At last, I was making progress. But, alas, just as I could see a way forward, it was cut short. Having reached the target in order to start CBT, this also meant that I was approaching the weight to be discharged. That should be good news, because I could be out, I could be free. But for me it was also bad news, because I discovered that as soon as I was discharged, I could no longer have the therapy sessions. I was devastated by this and so were my parents. At last, after such a long road, I was in a place with a person who could help me deal with the underlying issues, and this was to be taken away.

My parents did all they could to argue that I should remain at Leigh House. They knew that I had not reached the targets and had continued my deceptions. Despite all the hopes and promises of getting well I was still gripped by anorexia. However, on Wednesday 1st August 2007 I was discharged.

When any PEG left, all the other PEGs created a 'leaving book' in which they drew pictures, wrote poems and expressed their hopes and dreams for the person who was being discharged. Mine was beautifully made, with really poignant messages. I still have it, and I treasure it. Except that whenever I look at it, I am reminded of the devastating power of this dreadful disease.

To those who think that anorexia is a game, something to be flirted with or welcomed, I would say look in the leaving books of anyone who has been through it, see the lives that were stunted, the lives that were ruined, and the lives that were lost. Anorexia is a deadly disease. But it can be beaten.

A Letter To Myself After Discharge

Dear Lizzie,

I know that you have mixed feelings about coming to the end of this stage of medical care. You are pleased to be out, but you know that you are still not well. You know that, for many people, the front door of the hospital is a revolving door they will go through again. But you don't need to. You can get on with your life.

I know you felt a sense of safety and security in that tiny little hospital room. But that is not real life, and it is not the life for you. There is a big world out there, just waiting for you to step out and make a difference.

I wrote the following poem when I was in an inpatient hospital. I hope it will help you to break away from the downward spiral of anorexia. Don't look back, look forward.

Inside

It's a secret club
As life passes by
To eat or refuse?
Do we care if we die?

Because now we have lost
All sense of our life
Each meal is a battle
With trouble and strife

We eye up each other
Our food we compare
If one portion is bigger
We complain it's not fair

We pretend to eat
We say we're not lying
But we are empty and hollow
Inside, we are dying

Love

dizzie x

Chapter Seven
Transforming Disease

As I look back on my journey through anorexia, I recognise that there were three important sources of help that made a great difference to me: the professional care, my faith, and the support of my family. Regarding my family, without a doubt, one of the most important factors in my journey was the encouragement that my mum always provided. So many times she used to tell me, 'Lizzie, you *are* going to recover.' She believed in me. She affirmed me. She did everything she could to help me to see the future that was possible if I could beat this dreadful disease.

So it was that she booked theatre tickets for the very night I was discharged from Leigh House. This time it was the musical *Chitty Chitty Bang Bang*, and the lead role once again was played by Craig McLachlan. Mum knew that I would love the show because it was musical theatre. She wanted me to see immediately the wonderful possibilities for my life beyond anorexia. And she wanted to exorcise the demons of what happened last time I was in that theatre. Mum's hope was that on this evening out, I might reflect on how I was now in a much better place than I was when we went to see *White Christmas*. She hoped that, rather than moving backwards in my mind, as I had that time, I would now be encouraged to move forward and get on with my life. And I was. I wanted to be a new, healthy Lizzie. I wanted to put into practice some techniques I had learned from CBT. I wanted to conquer anorexia.

That night after the show, Mum hardly slept, as she prayed for me at this crucial stage. Would I go back to my old ways as too many did? Or would I keep moving forward to beat the disease? Then, in the early hours, she got up and did something unusual. She wrote a letter to Craig McLachlan. It was part of her own catharsis, rather like me writing a poem or painting some artwork. It was her way of marking some of the key points in my journey, and expressing her hope for my future. She told him some of my story, and how it had intersected with his. She told him about the switching on of the Christmas lights just before I was admitted to hospital. She told him about what happened at *White Christmas*, and of the very different celebration at *Chitty Chitty Bang Bang*. When she had finished, she sent it to him, care of the theatre. She wasn't expecting a reply, but the act of writing and sending it marked a moment for her. It helped her feel more positive for the future.

I was also feeling more positive. The CBT at Leigh House, even though it had been cut short, had been another significant stage in my journey. I wanted to be strong again. I wanted to be healthy. I wanted to work with the professionals and my family, and not against them.

I was no longer pressured into eating by the other PEGs sat around the table, I was at home with my parents, enjoying Mum's food. And I ate it. I was no longer sneaking around to find places to burn up calories, I was able to exercise sensibly with Mum or Dad. Mum started going swimming with me in the university pool. And Dad took me out for walks.

It was on those walks that Dad and I would talk and reflect. There was a phrase he had used many times in-between my time in hospital and Leigh House, when I was fighting particularly vigorously against food, and refusing to eat. He would say, 'Lizzie, when you win, you lose.' And he was right. Winning the battle to avoid a meal meant that I was losing more of my life to anorexia. But now things were looking different. Now I wanted to win against the anorexia. I wanted to do something worthwhile with my life.

It was while Dad and I were talking about this, eating a packed lunch on the top of Hengistbury Head in Dorset, on one of our father-daughter walks, that Mum got a phone call she hadn't expected. 'Hello, Carol,' an Australian voice said, 'it's Craig here.' He had been touched by the letter and invited me and Mum back to see the show again, with complimentary seats, and then to come for a chat in his dressing room afterwards. The night that we went, the cast were going out for a meal together, but he stayed behind and talked with me and Mum. He told me some of his story. He had a genuine humanity as he shared openly with me. And he encouraged me to keep on pressing on, to make the most of my life. I was fifteen years old. I had been stuck away in an inpatient unit for five months, and yet here was an apparently successful celebrity spending time with me, being open with me, and encouraging me. That moment meant a lot; it was another significant staging post on my journey.

September was now approaching and Suyog said that there was no problem with me going back to school. And there wasn't a problem with my weight or health. I was still struggling with the same thoughts and fears around food, but I was determined to overcome them, and I had the benefit of some effective CBT. So, physically, school was not an issue. Psychologically, however, it was a challenge. Once again I was to be the girl who had been away and was coming back. That hadn't worked out so well in the other school. Worse still, I had been away in a psychiatric hospital, which gave plenty of ammunition to any who wanted to be nasty to me.

However, the staff at Romsey School were absolutely brilliant. In particular, the pastoral support provided by the Head of Year Eleven, Debbie Stevenson, was a model of good practice. She liaised with CAMHS, she came to meetings at Brookvale, she made sure that there was joined up thinking between the health and educational services. She even let me eat my lunch with her in her office, while she talked with me about how I was coping.

But despite all this excellent support, I found it hard to cope with being back at school. I wanted to study – indeed I now had one year to do two year's work for my GCSEs – but my time in Leigh House had made me feel isolated from normal teenage life.

And being back in the hurly-burly of a big school was a shock to the system. This impacted my eating and, although I was fighting back against the anorexia as best I could, my weight began to drop. Within a few weeks, Suyog said that, once again, it wasn't safe for me to be at school.

Debbie Stevenson responded by arranging for me to have work sent home, where I could self-study. And that's what I did for the whole of that academic year. Mum and Dad arranged for a private English and maths tutor once a week, and my work was marked by teachers at the school, but apart from that I studied on my own at home. And I did work hard; I was determined to catch up and do the best I could in my GCSEs.

It was at this time that I also particularly valued the power of a moderated message board for people living with anorexia. This disease is very isolating in so many ways. The dishonesty and deception can cut you off from those closest to you. The consequences, as in my case, can be separation from school and other social environments. So, it is not surprising that many people living with anorexia turn to the web and social media. This can have a negative or a positive impact.

There are websites and networks, often referred to as 'pro-ana', 'pro-mia' or 'anamia', which seek to promote thinness, equating it with self-control and beauty, and often using quasi-spiritual messages to encourage users to strive for weight loss, endorsing it as a valid way of life. These are deeply dangerous.

But there are also websites and networks that can genuinely help those living through eating disorders, and the evidence shows that, properly run, they can have a significant positive impact. They can enable people to help themselves with or without clinical interventions. They circumvent the barriers that hinder people from seeking clinical help, and they allow the person to control their own support. In technical terms, they facilitate 'proactive self-care'.

One of these networks is the message boards run by the charity Beat. This is a forum providing asynchronous discussion in conversational threads. It is moderated by the Beat team to ensure that all posts are in line with their four published criteria: 'keeping safe online, posting mindfully, posting respectfully and posting responsibly'. And I found it immensely helpful, especially as I spent most of this year out of school.

Once again, as in my other positive experiences of professional support, the key was the genuine humanity of the people involved. The moderating team didn't act like cyber robots; they were real people who demonstrated a genuine compassion. In one of my early posts, I poured out my heart about the struggles I was experiencing at the time. I can't remember exactly what I said, but it clearly was inappropriate. In my desire to express myself I probably said things that would be unhelpful to others. So, of course, the moderators would not let it appear on the site. But they didn't just delete it and move on. In fact, they took the trouble to contact me directly, and talk with me. It made a real difference to my situation at that moment, and opened the door for many subsequent interactions online, as other people helped me. And I even began to help others.

This was another key moment of insight for me, as I began to see how the bad things that had happened in my life could be used for good in other people's lives. My dad had often expressed his belief about the relationship between faith and suffering. He said that, as he understands it 'God doesn't usually take away suffering, instead he transforms it into something far better than we could ever have imagined.' Now I was beginning to see how that could be possible in my life.

Indeed, Dad also helped me to recognise that no matter how weak you are, God can still use you to help others. He often talked about his own father's death. I never knew this grandfather, he died of cancer before I was born. His final weeks were spent at home, being cared for by friends and family who were nurses. One of these was my Aunty Gill, for whom faith had not been easy, but being with Dad's father as he died had a transformational impact on her. Shortly before he passed away, he said, 'Cry for yourselves, because you are going to miss me. But don't cry for me, because I am looking forward to going to be with God.' And his quiet, confident faith helped my aunty to move forward in her own faith.

In my work as a doctor I have cared for people as they are dying of cancer, and in those last hours they are extremely weak, as the body closes down. In fact, it is hard to imagine any greater frailty than that of a person in such a situation. And yet, in that position of extreme weakness, Dad's father had helped my aunty. My ongoing fragility, as I continued to struggle with the anorexia, was much less than my grandfather's. So, if God could use him to help others, surely he could use me too.

I developed an increasing passion to qualify as a doctor and to help others with eating disorders. I redoubled my efforts at my study, because I knew that my GCSE results would be important as I went on to A Levels and applied to medical schools. By the end of my GCSE years I had taken eight subjects and achieved all As and A-stars. Without a doubt, much of this was due to the support that Romsey School provided for me. And it was a special extra joy, at the prize-giving ceremony at the end of the year, to be awarded the Shield of Endeavour, which was given each year to someone who had overcome particular challenges. However, I felt that it really should be me giving them an award, rather than the other way around.

Coinciding with the GCSE exams, my relationship with Beat took a new turn. Having derived huge benefit from their moderated message boards, I applied to be a Beat Ambassador, a new scheme they had just launched. As an ambassador one of my roles was to facilitate live chats, which gave me opportunities to help other individuals. But the ambassador role also enabled me to play my part in advocating for improvements in services for all people living through eating disorders.

One of these was the opportunity to speak at a special event in Downing Street, at the home of the Chancellor of the Exchequer. This was a whole new world for me, and not one with which I was at all familiar. Having passed through security I tried to look as confident as possible as I walked along Downing Street. I felt better when I noticed something I recognised. I had seen that door, with its famous number 10, on many news reports. So, I marched up and knocked, only to be told by the very polite doorman that I had got the wrong house – I should be next door. Still, I picked myself up, went to the right building and found myself in a room filled with the 'great and the good', which was rather overawing for a sixteen-year-old girl.

Passionate about making an impact for those I was representing, I knew I must launch in and start talking to people. I spotted a man stood on his own, off to the side, so I approached him and, as confidently as I could I said, 'Hello, what brings you here?' Smiling, he replied, 'I live here.' I didn't know what the Chancellor looked like – I knew very little about politics – but I did know from my own experience about the dreadful disease of anorexia, and now I had an opportunity to share this directly with the man who, I later discovered, held the country's purse strings.

This was followed by opportunities to speak at events in the Houses of Parliament, the Royal College of Nursing, and eventually on *BBC Breakfast*. It was this TV appearance that I found most challenging. Not because the interviewers were difficult, they were absolutely lovely (as you can see if you watch the video on LifeHurts.net). It was because my struggles with anorexia would now be exposed to a new group of friends.

Two months before, in September 2009, I had started A Level courses at Peter Symonds College in Winchester. It was a train journey from my home in Southampton and it gave me an opportunity to start all over with new people. Here I would not be known as 'the girl with anorexia'. I could just be myself. No-one need be told anything about my past. I could focus on my future.

Agreeing to be interviewed on *BBC Breakfast* was certainly going to let the cat out of the bag. But I knew I had to do it. How else was I going to advocate for better services for people living with eating disorders if I was not prepared to put my head above the parapet and be open about my own story? And, surely, trying to hide my past would make me complicit in the continuance of the stigma around mental health.

So I agreed to take part in the programme, and I spoke as honestly as I could about my journey through anorexia. I talked about the ways in which I had been helped, by my family and by professionals.

As I travelled back on the train towards Winchester, I wondered how the people at my new college would react to me now.

A Letter To Myself After Telling My Story Publicly

Dear Lizzie,

Stigma breeds fear. But it can be overcome with courage and honesty.

I understand why you would rather that people didn't hear about your history of mental health issues. You don't want to be known as 'the girl with anorexia'. You just want to be accepted for who you are. And that's right. You are a person with a future, not just a patient with a medical record.

But you are also a person living in the community of this world. And you have the opportunity to do something to break down the stigma of mental health. If you are willing to be open and honest, you can make a difference.

And do you know what? When you are open about the challenges you have faced, you will find that many other people will be honest about theirs. Because there are no perfect people. Life hurts for everyone.

So, when you speak out, you might be surprised at the reaction you get, and the impact you have, enabling others to stand up with courage and honesty, which will break down stigma and fear.

Love,

Lizzie x

Chapter Eight
Institutional Stigma

People and cultures develop over time. Attitudes change, and that has certainly been evident in relation to the stigma attached to mental health. But that change is not uniform, and pockets of prejudice continue. In my experience, these tend to be more institutional than individual. As I progressed through college to medical school I found that there were still elements of stigma and prejudice within the way that institutions operated. However, wonderfully, I also found that individuals were increasingly sympathetic to the challenges of living with an eating disorder.

Having been worried about what my new friends at Sixth Form college would say when they discovered my history of anorexia, I was delighted with their response to my BBC interview. They were encouraging and supportive. Indeed, this led to the deepening of many relationships. My dad often said that 'true friendships develop when people are frank about failures, not when they show off successes.' I certainly discovered the truth of this in my time at college and then on into medical school, where I developed relationships with a depth and honesty that I had previously never thought possible. These friends and colleagues have learned to understand and appreciate what it is like to live with an eating disorder, and I have learned to understand and appreciate the various different challenges that they also experience in their own lives. The fact is that life hurts for all of us, just in different ways.

This has continued into my current role as a hospital doctor. Even now, there are many people who help and support me, and have accommodated the ongoing challenges that I face. They are enabling me to continue my journey through anorexia, and to utilise the insights that it brings into my developing role in medicine.

However, along the way, I have also seen examples of what my dad has referred to as an 'institutional memory of historical stigma'. That is, in some institutions, although individuals may have long since rejected the stigma, there remains some inherent stigmatising assumptions within the processes and structures by which the institution operates. In medicine, for example, there was a time when doctors were expected to present a perfect picture of health, as if they were to be their own adverts for the effectiveness of their medicine. The ancient proverb 'physician heal thyself' carries with it an implicit assumption that we can only be effective as doctors if we have healed ourselves. So, weaknesses and problems in our own health would disqualify us from practising medicine.

I first noticed this when various advisors within school and college sought to dissuade me from my goal of medical school. They told me that the health challenges I had experienced would prevent me from being an effective doctor.

In a subtle, but also more troubling, way I also saw this in a keynote lecture on a medicine taster day that I attended at Nottingham University. Together with a number of friends from college, who were all hoping to apply for medicine, I had travelled up to Nottingham the evening before and stayed overnight in a hall of residence. We were all very excited as it felt like we were getting our first taste of the university experience. The taster day was really helpful as we learned about different course structures, and got an overview of life in medical school. But we were also repeatedly told about the pressure, stresses and strains that a medical student experiences.

In that context, we were given a big set-piece presentation by a doctor from a first-response team. He had obviously given this talk many times before, and he came equipped with a video showing multiple examples of real life medical emergencies such as car accidents and major traumas. All of them showed explicit scenes of horrific injuries experienced by real people. Understandably, his presentation was a shock to the entire audience of fresh-faced seventeen year olds. And he clearly intended that. After three people had fainted, he turned it off, saying that he only ever played it until three had collapsed. That day he turned it off after just a few minutes.

I was shocked and appalled by this presentation. Of course, I shared the same shock as the rest of the audience at the injuries we had seen. But what appalled me was the implicit assumption from his presentation that if any of us found such scenes too upsetting, then medicine was not for us.

I thought back to my experiences of health professionals who had cared for me through my illness. Those who helped me the most were those who held on to their humanity. They didn't distance themselves from my pain by a shield of professionalism. They cared, they felt, they empathised. If that doctor had intended to put off someone like me, with the weaknesses that I knew only too well, then it had the very opposite effect. I became even more determined that I wanted to get to medical school and qualify as a doctor. And, if I did, then I wanted to bring into my medicine the extra empathy and humanity that had developed in my heart and mind because of my journey through anorexia.

I knew that this would not be easy. And, indeed, in my first few weeks at medical school I experienced again the persistence of that institutional stigma in a way that nearly stopped me altogether. But before I share that moment with you, let me fill in what happened in-between.

My determination to get on with my life, study medicine, and make a difference in the world, enabled me to fight back against the intrusive thoughts and fears that I still experienced around food. Throughout my sixth form years I continued to have meetings with Suyog, but these had become increasingly light touch as he simply monitored the fact that I was eating enough to stay sufficiently healthy to continue at college.

My family sustained me with their great support, as did my faith, which was becoming increasingly integrated into my life. Soon after starting my A Levels I decided to move churches, away from the one that my parents attended, striking out on my own. I had heard a lot about Above Bar Church in Southampton and believed that here was somewhere that would help me to study the Bible for myself. And it did.

One of the ministers was a wonderful guy called Andrew Page, who was an old friend of my parents. I found him to be one of the best Bible teachers I had ever known. He didn't have a dramatic rhetorical style, quite the opposite in fact, he just talked like a real person. And he had a really gentle and gracious ability to point his listeners away from himself, into the text of the Bible. Through Andrew I learned to engage with Scripture for myself, and to think about my developing faith.

It was also at this church that I first saw a boy, about my age, called Giles McNaught. We were in a meeting of about twenty young people, talking together about faith. I remember looking at him as he spoke. I recall thinking how amazing he was, but I thought that nothing would ever happen between us because he was far too popular to be interested in someone like me. Still, we talked together as friends and started messaging each other over Facebook.

It wasn't until the summer at the end of my sixth form, just after I had taken my A Levels, that I realised there could be more to this than just friendship. We were away at a summer camp and we spent increasing amounts of time together. We talked about our faith, we read the Bible together, and we shared our thoughts. The relationship deepened and some weeks later, just before he went off to university in Bath and I started my gap year, he asked me to be his girlfriend. It would be another five years before we got married, but I can honestly say that I don't know how I would have got through that time without him. Because I continued to struggle with food, and despite all the ups and downs of my journey through anorexia, Giles stood by me through it all, and he still does. He loves me unconditionally, like God does. I don't take that lightly. I have not been easy for him.

Those who had tried to put me off medicine did not succeed, but they had led me to decide that I should apply for a deferred place at university, so that I could take a gap year. I submitted applications to four medical schools and got called for three interviews. The one at King's College London was particularly traumatic and, to this day, I still don't know if it showed another example of the persistence of institutional stigma, or a very clever interview technique.

In my personal statement on my application, I had been very open and honest about my struggles. I said that, in common with many who live with anorexia, I set myself high standards and tend to be a perfectionist. As soon as the interview started, the first question, posed in an accusatorial tone, was something like: 'With your weaknesses why on earth do you think you'd be strong enough to do this? And if you are such a perfectionist, surely you will struggle with the fact that you can never be a perfect doctor.' I was really shocked. But I pushed back and replied that, if someone in my family was ill, I'd rather that their doctor was a perfectionist than someone who would settle for anything less than the best. More questions followed, but my mind kept tracking back to that first one, and I don't remember anything else about the interview, except that afterwards I ran to the toilets and bawled my eyes out. I had set my heart on King's because it was such a good medical school, with so many experts on the teaching staff, and I was now convinced that they would never take me.

But I was wrong – they did offer me a place, as did the other two schools. I accepted the place at King's, with the deferred entry, and started planning my gap year. I wanted to take time to continue overcoming the intrusive thoughts and fears about food, and I wanted to do that by spending more time developing my faith. I knew that if I could really see myself as God saw me, and love myself as he loves me, then this could provide a major breakthrough.

My dad had told me about a residential study centre not far from our home. He knew the people who ran it; he had lectured there on several occasions. It specialises in helping people in their late teens and twenties to think through questions of faith, with no pressure, just an opportunity to think, question and explore. Dad said that, as he understood it, they were particularly helpful for people who struggled with mental health issues. So, I contacted them and arranged to go there for an initial couple of weeks, with a view to spending a much longer time if it worked out.

Unfortunately, it didn't. They clearly had very little understanding of the challenges faced by people who are living through an eating disorder. The daily programme consisted of individual study, which was great, and conversations with the team, which were wonderful. But the central focus of the community was the meals, three times a day, when everyone gathered to eat and talk together. High calorie, stodgy meals were provided and these were plated up in large portions and placed in front of each of us around a big communal table.

The leaders had probably not realised the problem that large plated meals like this would pose to someone who was living through an eating disorder, and the way that this would trigger distressing and intrusive thoughts and fears – the very things that I had gone there to deal with. It wouldn't have taken much for the experience to have been very different. Just providing the food on a serve-yourself buffet table, with lower-calorie options such as salads, would have done it. But that wasn't available, and within a few days I couldn't take it any more. I told them I had to leave.

At a time when so many people are experiencing eating disorders, I appeal to all community groups to recognise the challenges we face. It is wonderful that society has made all sorts of provision for a wide range of disabilities. Community venues have wheelchair access for disabled, signing for deaf, audio description for visually impaired, and so the list goes on. It is only another simple step to ensure that food-based activities recognise the challenges faced by those living with eating disorders.

I now suddenly had to make alternative plans for my gap year. Thankfully, because my parents ran an educational charity that they had founded, they quickly agreed for me to volunteer with their team. And I had a job in the box office at the nearby university theatre to be able to pay my way. As it turned out, I had a great year with many opportunities to play my part in making a difference in the world. In particular, I got involved with the Global Student Forum, a development education project which my mum and dad had initiated, funded by the Department for International Development. And I went to the European Leadership Forum in Hungary, where both Mum and Dad were speaking, and where, thankfully, all the food was served buffet-style with lower-calorie options.

The year soon passed, and time came for me to go to King's to start at medical school. I vividly remember the journey to London, squeezed in the back of the car, surrounded by boxes of clothes and books. Mum and Dad took me to my room in the hall of residence, and Freshers' Week began.

There were lots of activities designed for people to get to know one another. But, unfortunately, most of them were geared around food and drink, which immediately raised again my intrusive thoughts and fears. I spent much of the week trying to avoid situations where I would struggle. It was not a happy time. And I think there will have been challenges for many other students with all sorts of different mental health issues. It seemed as if the organisers assumed that all students are naturally happy, gregarious people who love to eat lots of food and get drunk. Certainly, many are in that mould, but many more are not. As someone who was brought up in a family that was always determined to be inclusive, and provide opportunities for all types of people, I felt like I did not fit.

However, it was only a week, and I tried to focus my mind on the beginning of the course, which was why I had come. I went to the first lecture with the girl in the room next to mine, who was also studying medicine. We were slightly late and so we sat towards the back of the lecture hall. It was the only time I ever sat at the back.

I vividly remember how I felt in the first few lectures. I was so excited to be there. What a privilege it was to have these medical experts at King's willing to teach me. I knew that I wanted to be the best possible doctor, and that I never wanted to be in a situation where I couldn't properly help a patient because I hadn't learned fully about that aspect of medicine. So, I wanted to learn everything I could. And there was a lot to learn! I worked very hard.

However, the impact of Freshers' Week, and the pressure of the constant studying took its toll on my mind. When you live with anorexia, times of stress can reawaken thought patterns that you assumed had been conquered. The fear of eating was returning very powerfully. After living with anorexia since my early teenage years, without the underlying issues being resolved, there were well-established thought patterns that so readily reasserted themselves. If I couldn't control my study, then I would control my eating and start once more seriously restricting my food intake. Despite all the advances that I had made over the past few years, I seemed powerless to resist that thought pattern.

A few days later, Dad happened to be coming to London for meetings and I called him to ask if he would come to see me. Of course, he was delighted. As soon as I saw him I broke down in tears and told him that I was really struggling. And I was. I was struggling with the study, but most of all I was struggling again with the anorexia.

He took me out to the pub opposite the hall of residence and sat with me at a table outside, in the autumn sunshine. He asked me to describe what the work was like. I explained that we had lectures solidly from 9 a.m. to 5 p.m. Many students skipped them, but I was at every one; since these medical experts were willing to teach me, there was no way I was going to miss them. We had an hour off for lunch, but instead of eating I went back to my room to study. Then, in the evening, when others went out to eat and drink, I might only nibble on some carrots while I read the textbook sections on the day's lectures and tried to make sense of what I had heard. And that went on late into the night, before I headed back to the lectures the next morning, without any breakfast.

In a very gentle way, Dad didn't tackle the eating head on, but instead invited me to think of a different way of learning which might mean that I felt more in control of the studying, and therefore less vulnerable to the resurgent desire to control my food intake. Instead of reading the textbooks in the evening after the lectures, he suggested reading them the night before, so that I could, in my own way, get to grips with the subject of the lecture. Then listening to the lecturer would be easier, because it was essentially recapping what I already knew. And I could ask the lecturer informed questions about issues that I didn't yet understand.

This made sense, and I thought that it could work. After all, I had self-studied before and had strategies for doing this. But it meant that I had to get ahead of the lectures, and I already felt that I was falling behind. My confidence ebbed and flowed as we talked. At one moment I thought I could do it, at another I thought that I never would. At one moment I thought that the anorexia would not blight my life once again, at another it seemed inevitable.

So, Dad suggested that I set myself a manageable goal. Try it through this term and see how I did in the exams at the end. If my marks were low, then I could rethink. But if they were alright, then I had a strategy for the rest of the course. As Dad left I felt really confident again. I could do this.

And in the open and honest way that I had been brought up, I wrote to a lecturer to share with them how I had been struggling, but that I now had a strategy. I told them about the challenges I was experiencing, with the warning signs of the resurgence of anorexia, and how I intended to overcome it again. I thought that sharing this information, and this strategy, might enable me to access any additional support that might be available for students living with an eating disorder.

I wasn't prepared for the response that I received almost immediately. They emailed straight back to say that if I was facing challenges like this, at this stage of the course, then medicine clearly wasn't for me, and I should leave immediately. I don't blame them for this reply. They probably made it instinctively as the persistence of institutional stigma meant that this was their 'go-to' response. If I was facing health problems, then I should leave. I felt devastated.

A Letter To Myself After
Being Told I Should Leave

Dear Lizzie,

I know you feel hurt by what has happened. I understand that you feel devastated to see how the stigma about mental health still persists in institutions.

But you know that many individuals have an increasingly enlightened attitude. And institutions are made up of individuals. Many of them want things to change, just as much as you do.

So, stand firm. Do not give up. Fight for the right to achieve, don't submit to the assumption of failure.

And as you do, you will be one more individual, joining together with others, to see the eventual eradication of institutionalised stigma.

Love,

Lizzie x

Chapter Nine
Recovery?

There's a traditional saying that 'time is a great healer.' Like many old clichés it sounds lovely, and it is well meant by those who say it to someone who is in pain. But it isn't really true.

Healing requires action. Something must be done. If my car gets a flat tyre while I am driving to the hospital, it is no good me sitting in it quietly saying, 'Time is a great healer.' No matter how long I wait, the tyre will not recover. I have to change the wheel and take it to a garage to get the puncture mended.

Of course, the human body is more than a lifeless machine like a car. In us, things do change if left alone, but what appears to be healing over time may actually create more problems for the future. Imagine that you fall and break your arm, but you don't come to the hospital. As long as you can manage the pain, it may well appear to heal. In an initial fracture a haematoma will develop, followed by inflammation as new blood vessels grow and granulation tissue is laid down. New bone matrix will form and remodeling will take place. The bone may have 'healed' itself but probably with non-union or malunion. And months or years later you will experience complications such as contractures and osteoarthritis. To avoid these complications, some action would have to be taken by medical professionals. The broken bone would have to be realigned.

After I left Leigh House, having had only a few weeks of professionally delivered CBT, I was determined to get on with my life, to make a difference in the world. I was set resolutely on getting to medical school and qualifying as a doctor. And, over the time that followed, the intrusive thoughts and fears about food did start to fade in my mind, so that I was able to eat enough to survive and function. That was good. And like dealing with the flat tyre, it didn't happen on its own. It was because I was using my determination positively, rather than negatively.

However, rather like leaving a broken bone to mend itself, this didn't mean that I was properly healed. The underlying issues had not been resolved in the early days of my development of anorexia, in fact, they went on to form established thought patterns, which rendered me vulnerable to a resurgence at times of stress.

I certainly was stressed in my first few weeks at medical school, and even more so when the lecturer had suggested that I should leave. But I wasn't about to give up. I decided that I would push through, and use the strategy that my dad had outlined. This did make a difference to my studying.

I also talked to my tutor about the fact that I seemed to read much more slowly than other people. I was immediately referred to Learning Support and very soon had a test which revealed my dyslexia. This was followed by all sorts of excellent support facilities from King's so that this challenge could be overcome.

Meanwhile, the challenges that continued because I was still living with anorexia were immensely helped by fellow students. On that first day of the course, when I had arrived late and sat at the back of the lecture hall, I had been amongst the other latecomers. I was shocked that some of them seemed more intent on talking to one another than listening to the medical experts who were teaching us. A few weeks later, in the same lecture hall, these students were again talking together, and I got so cross that I turned around to one of the chatterers behind me, gave her an intense stare and told her to 'shush'. Little did I know at that time that this girl, called Vidya, would become one of my best friends, one of my greatest supporters in living through anorexia, and indeed my clinical partner through medical school.

Vidya and I developed a closeness characterised by 'tough love'.

I would lovingly chastise her by pointing out that, if she wanted to be a doctor, she couldn't turn up late for lectures. And she would lovingly chastise me by telling me that, if I wanted to be a doctor, I would have to eat properly to have the strength for the course.

But it wasn't just words, it was action too. One of my favourite photos of us together as clinical partners is the selfie we took on the day we first put on scrubs to go into the operating theatre. We were really excited at this next step forward in our medical training. She wasn't late that day! But unfortunately I was still struggling with overpowering thoughts and fears about food, and I hadn't eaten much for several days. So, as we stood in the heat of the operating theatre, I felt increasingly weak and faint, my vision became cloudy and I could feel myself falling to the floor. Vidya caught me and took me out of the room. She didn't stop there. Despite the fact that she was so excited to have her first experience of the operating theatre, she pulled off her scrubs and took me home, right across London, made sure that I had something to eat, put me in bed, and only then returned to the hospital.

Each day, Vidya would join me to walk to lecture halls or hospitals. She would talk to me about how I was getting on with food. She would pray with me and encourage me. I will be forever grateful for the help that she provided throughout my years at medical school.

Meanwhile, my boyfriend Giles also provided wonderful long-distance support. He was reading history in Bath, but he would Skype me every evening to talk. And sometimes, when we had finished chatting, we just left the Skype video on so that we could see each other as we studied. Knowing that he was there made such a difference to me. Here was someone, beyond my family, who had chosen to care for me, despite all my faults and all my problems. Even when I hated myself, he still loved me.

Understanding anorexia has been a real journey for Giles, as it is for anyone who has never lived with it. Looking from the outside there are so many aspects of this disease that just don't seem to make sense. Even on the inside there are features that suddenly take you by surprise.

The various different forms of eating disorders are sometimes referred to under the umbrella name of 'chaotic eating', and that can be a helpful term. For me, as with many people living with anorexia who then force themselves to eat, I suddenly started binge eating. Within the community of people living with anorexia, binge eating is the ugly unspoken secret.

After so many years of restricting my food intake, here I was away from home, knowing that I had to consume food in order to continue with my medical studies, and suddenly finding a thrill from eating. Physiologically, the food released endorphins that made me feel better. And so I continued to eat, and eat and eat. Living in a communal environment this meant that I embarrassingly sometimes ate other people's food from the fridge, because once I started I could not stop until I felt so full that I had to make myself sick, which also released more endorphins that made me feel even better.

I am so thankful that Giles and Vidya were patient and understanding. They helped me to cope. They enabled me to function, despite the persistence of the underlying thought patterns that had become so deeply entrenched in my mind.

So, I was able to continue with my studies, and I worked hard. At the end of the first two years, I passed the preclinical exams, and moved on to the three years of clinical training. This involved rotations in various different hospital departments across London and the South East, where Vidya and I would support each other. I brought her coffee in the morning to ensure that she got out of bed on time, and she supported me during the day by ensuring that I ate sufficiently. The placements brought wonderful opportunities to learn more medicine, and develop some clinical skills. It was very exciting to see how I would be able to serve people once I qualified. My life was well and truly back on track. But I was still not free from the intrusive thoughts and fears associated with food, which could be set off in all sorts of unexpected ways.

One such trigger occurred when Giles asked me to marry him. What a wonderful day that was, and he was so romantic in the way that he proposed. I could never describe the sheer thrill that I experienced when I heard the words, 'Will you marry me, until death do us part?' My thoughts immediately went to the wedding, as it must for many girls in this situation, and I pictured myself in a beautiful white dress, walking down the aisle towards him. But then almost instantly my mind was filled with fear. People would be looking at me, and photos would be taken that would last a lifetime. Immediately I thought that I must lose weight, and lose it fast. When you are living through anorexia, even the greatest moments can suddenly trigger your worst fears.

I tried to fight back against these thoughts. I desperately didn't want the anorexia to take back my mind, my life, my future. I would like to say that by now, as I was so far through my medical degree, I had gained the insight and strength to brush those fears aside. But I couldn't. And the months that followed were a constant battle that blighted the wedding preparations.

Still, I kept focused on my studies and tried to control my fears. And on 12th September 2015, just before I started my final year at medical school, I married Giles in a wonderful service at my parents' church, which was full of friends and family who had supported me, and prayed for me, for so long. Andrew Page, the minister from my church who had helped me so much in my journey of faith, gave a wonderful sermon about selfless commitment.

Dad was very emotional that day. I know that a bride often cries, and so does the bride's mother, but I don't think that many dads cry. However, as he walked me down the aisle, and he tried to smile, tears ran down my dad's cheeks. It wasn't until afterwards that he told me why. When I had been very ill, Dad had experienced terrible repeated nightmares that woke him up on many occasions. He dreamed he was walking with me down the aisle of the church. He said that, in his nightmare, he was always seeing it from above, watching himself walk slowly with me. But I wasn't in a wedding dress, I was in a coffin, having died from this dreadful disease.

So, on that beautiful, bright September day, as we took our first steps down the aisle together, Dad simply could not hold back the tears. When we reached the front, and Dad sat down next to Mum, they were delighted that I was starting on a new chapter of my life, with the man I love, and who had already shown how much he loves me.

We would be together again at another big event a year later, as Mum, Dad and Giles joined me for my graduation from medical school. It was a wonderfully happy occasion, in Southwark Cathedral, as I gathered with all my colleagues to receive our medical degrees. Here I was, the girl whose life had been blighted by anorexia, the girl who could so easily have died when she was fourteen, the girl who had to catch up at school to replace the time lost in hospitals, the girl whom the medical school had suggested should leave after the first few days. Now, I was qualifying as a doctor.

Our names were read out in alphabetical order, as we each went forward to collect our certificates. But when they called mine they also announced something more. I had not only qualified, but I had also been awarded the Legg Prize in Surgery for achieving the highest mark in the written exams. It was lovely to hear my friends and family applaud and cheer. But I wanted to applaud them, because this had only been possible because of their love and support. And I was only able to embark on my medical career because of the help that had been given to me by so many medical professionals over the years. Whatever I am able to achieve, and whomever I am able to help in the future, it will truly have been a team effort.

So, this is my story, my personal journey through anorexia. I know that stories are meant to have a beginning, a middle and an end; and I would have liked my ending to tell you that I am now fully recovered, that I have no overpowering thoughts about food or weight anymore, no negative cognitions about myself, and that my life is great. But I can't tell you that. Life hurts. And it is still hurting for me now. I guess that life hurts for all of us, whatever our own personal journey. But I know that I want to live it.

For me, the path to living through anorexia started with knowing that I have a choice, and being determined to take it. It hasn't been an easy road and I'm still on it. There are many times, even now, when I seem to take two steps backwards for every one step forward. I am constantly frustrated at how long this journey takes. It is slow and painful; it takes continued determination.

Staying alive, and knowing that I want to fight for recovery, was made possible by professional help, my supportive family and friends, and my faith in God. Full recovery will take more time and more work, if it is even possible. Eating disorders come in different forms, and although I look a healthy weight right now as this book is published, that doesn't mean that my thoughts are any more healthy than they were when I obviously looked very ill.

I don't think it is possible to define what is full recovery from an eating disorder, as it varies from person to person. But I do know what full recovery would mean for me. Full recovery would not just be eating and being at a healthy weight. It would be knowing, without a doubt, that I am totally loved and accepted for who I am, not for what I look like or what others think of me. It would be no longer using food to control my emotions. It would be choosing to eat whatever I want, and enjoy it, without any intrusive thoughts or fears.

I don't know if that will ever be possible for me, because the thought patterns became so entrenched in my mind through the early years in which I never received effective therapy to deal with the underlying issues. But what I do know is that, even if it is too late for me, I will use all the time and energy that God gives me to help others to avoid the devastating impact of anorexia in their lives, and in the lives of those they love.

I am certain that education is vital. We must enable friends and family to spot the early signs of anorexia so that they can take appropriate steps to help those who are just starting down the road of this dreadful disease. And I am certain that the right type of early intervention is crucial. We must ensure that effective therapy is available, as soon as possible, to help people deal with the thought patterns that drive them to lose weight.

I am still on my journey. Life still hurts, but I want to live it to the full and make a positive difference in the lives of other people.

Epilogue

Reassess

I don't know what to call you
You have morphed so many times
You used to be my friend
I wish I'd read between the lines

I cannot go back now
But I know that I have hope
You have taken so much from me
You thought I couldn't cope

I will laugh at you in my joy
And I will laugh at you in my sorrow
How dare you take so much from me
And rob me of tomorrow?

I don't know what the future holds
And I dare not even guess
But my prayer is that, going forward
Who you pick on, they will reassess...

Appendix 1
A Father's Perspective

It was the phone call that every father dreads: 'You have to come back, Lizzie's in hospital and it's serious.' My wife, Carol, was obviously distressed, so I immediately cancelled my meetings and started the journey home, getting to the hospital early the next morning with flowers in my hand and fear in my heart. The doctors took me aside and warned me that my fourteen-year-old daughter's vital signs were so low that she was in danger. In fact, her illness was life threatening. They told me that it would take some time to get her stable, and I should expect a long road to recovery beyond that.

That certainly was a wake-up call to me. Carol had been deeply concerned about Lizzie's restriction of her food intake for many months, but I had held on to the hope that it would simply pass.

But now the extent of Lizzie's illness was clearly evident. And so, I swung into action. I was used to solving problems and making things happen, and anorexia, I assumed, was just another problem that I could solve. So, I asked the doctors what their treatment would be and how long it would take. Their answers were vague, which I interpreted as evasive. I've since realised that anorexia is a complex multi-factorial illness that no-one fully understands, and no-one can cure with a simple treatment.

Over the months and years that followed, while Lizzie battled against this illness, I had to make major changes in my attitude and approach. It wasn't easy. Nor is it easy for many other fathers of children living with anorexia. As I got to know other dads in the inpatient unit to which Lizzie was later admitted, I discovered that many of us were action-focused, solution-driven people. Perhaps that is why many of our children were high-achieving perfectionists, which made them vulnerable to this dreadful disease?

I will be eternally grateful for the work of the family therapists, Dave and Elaine, who spent many hours helping us as a family to consider how we could support Lizzie as she lived through her eating disorder.

First, I had to let go of my simplistic reaction to anorexia, which I have since discovered is prevalent amongst many when they first encounter this disease. 'What's the problem with you eating?' I would say to Lizzie. 'There's food. Your hands work. Your mouth works. Just eat it!' I am so thankful that my daughter has forgiven me for my crass ignorance.

Then, I had to develop an understanding of what we could achieve together. For me, it is probably best summed up by an illustration I often used when talking about how we, as a family, were seeking to help Lizzie. I used to say it was like we were all in a rowing boat, trying to get up a river. And, while I was pulling hard on the oars, I would look around to see that Lizzie was rowing in the opposite direction. So, as a solution-driven person, I felt betrayed and angry. But as I began to understand more about eating disorders, and what was going on in Lizzie's mind, it suddenly struck me that I was focusing on the wrong goal. Instead of trying to get up the river, my focus should be on keeping us all together in the boat. I should be patient if we went downstream for a while. I should be understanding if Lizzie was going through a particularly difficult patch and was losing the will to conquer her illness. What mattered was that we were all together in the boat.

I couldn't make Lizzie fight back against her illness. I had to love her and respect her. I had to stay with her and support her as she battled with her thoughts and fears. Yes, there were times when Carol and I, and the doctors, had to step in and take action to save Lizzie from doing irreparable harm to herself. But ultimately, it was Lizzie who had the lead role in fighting this disease. I was just a supporting actor.

For dads who are used to being in control of their professional lives, and tend to act the same in their family lives, this is a very hard adjustment to make. I had to change from leading her on, to cheering her on. And gradually, through professional help, her strong faith, and the appropriate support that we as a family learned to provide, Lizzie found the hope and strength to overcome. She even continued her education, secured a place at medical school, and is now a hospital doctor. Lizzie still struggles with food and the underlying issues that led to her eating disorder, but she is alive, and healthy, and making a positive difference in the lives of others.

Nick Pollard (Lizzie's father)

Appendix 2
A Mother's Perspective

When I first held her in my arms in the maternity unit, I knew that I would love her with all of my heart. I wanted to help her to fulfil her potential to make a difference in the world.

Throughout the pregnancy I had done everything I could to help her grow a strong, healthy body. And I continued this as she developed from a baby to a toddler. There I was, looking out for her every step, guiding and encouraging her in every way. Soon she blossomed into a beautiful girl with a strong will, a fierce courage and great resilience. I remember her learning to ride a bike. After countless hours of failed attempts, with me calling out, 'Cycle through the wobbles,' at last she took off on her own, with a determination to catch up with her elder brother. I remember her learning to do the monkey bars at the play area. Hour after hour she tried but fell off into the sand, only to get straight back up to try again until eventually she mastered it.

But now that she was fourteen, and gripped by the ravages of anorexia and self-harm, where was she now? Was she still behind those sunken eyes that longed for peace that never came? Was she within the scars that were seared on her arms and legs like gaping rips across a beautiful picture? Was she behind the flashes of hate when I gave her food that I had lovingly prepared? Was she within the fierce resolve to refuse absolutely all the nourishment I offered? I didn't know where she was anymore. But I knew that I had become her enemy.

My instinct had always been to nurture and protect her. But how could I nurture her when she refused all food? And how could I protect her from herself? The beautiful body I had grown in the warmth of my womb, was now cold, malnourished and scarred. The sweet nature of this loving, generous daughter was now deceptive and self-focused, overwhelmed by the power of anorexia. How could I ever help her to find her way out of her own personal hell?

When you care for someone who is living with anorexia, you have to develop a tough skin. Of course you still cry and hurt. But you have to keep going no matter what they throw at you. When they hate you, you love them back. When they throw food at you, you prepare more. When they lie to you and deceive you about food or exercise, you become wise to their tricks and techniques. You have to decide when to challenge and when to step back, but they have to know that you are always there.

Through God's goodness, I managed to hold on to my faith that inside this dreadfully broken Lizzie was still the real person, my beautiful loving and determined daughter. And it was Lizzie's determination that was one of the keys that I kept offering to her as I tried to help her find release from this dreadful disease.

Lizzie knew that her determination could be used for good. Like the time she made literally hundreds of Red Nose Day cakes to raise money at school for Comic Relief. And the way she pushed herself to run or cycle to raise money for many other charities. Tragically, this determination had now been hijacked by anorexia and was driving her relentless self-destruction. But I believed that she could turn it around. And I tried to help her believe that too.

Whether in hospital or community care, Lizzie and I spent many hours together talking, challenging, crying, hugging as I tried to encourage her to use her powerful determination for good again, rather than harm. We talked about what she could achieve in her life if she would fight back and defeat the anorexia. We talked about how she could make a difference in the world. Each conversation slowly turned the direction of her determination, until gradually she began to take small positive steps forward.

Tragically, there are many other mothers who are facing, or have faced, the same challenge with their children. What is my advice to these mothers? Keep on loving, keep on praying, keep on giving. And keep on encouraging them that they can beat this illness. Even though it may not feel like it at the moment, know that there is light at the end of the tunnel, there is a hope and a future.

Carol Pollard (Lizzie's mother)

Appendix 3
Family Impact

In 2005 researchers published the results of research which investigated the impact that a child living with anorexia nervosa had upon their families (Whitney et al., 2005). The study was conducted with parents of patients in the eating disorder unit in the South London and Maudsley NHS Trust. Twenty fathers and twenty mothers were asked, during their family integrated treatment, to write a reflective letter describing what it is like for them to have a child who is living with anorexia. These reflections were then analysed to identify any common themes.

Both mothers and fathers blamed themselves for their child's illness and they often questioned what they could have done differently in bringing up their child to have prevented this. One father is quoted as saying, 'I feel guilty because I must have influenced this illness in some way; it is inevitable as a parent that I could have been in a position to do something to have helped her sooner'. The parents also reported that they felt failures and inadequate, hopeless and powerless about the future. These feelings of guilt and shame are not new and are well recognised in people caring for someone with an eating disorder (Treasure et al., 2001).

Another theme that emerged was how both parents often felt highly manipulated by their child's illness, and that they felt as if they were being controlled. As a result they often had a much more dependent relationship with that child, who demanded great amounts of their time.

In addition, both mothers and fathers viewed the illness as a chronic, lifelong condition, and often felt this was something from which their child would never recover, and that they would never be able to adjust again to normal life. They both expressed anger at the stigma associated with eating disorders.

Themes that were prominent in the mothers specifically, included that they were often highly emotional about the situation; they reported a great deal of sadness about their child being unwell, and the resultant missed opportunities. Their deep emotional response had physical effects, with them often experiencing sleep deprivation and exhaustion. One mother was recorded as saying, 'So how does a mother feel? Failed, useless, bad, stupid, guilty, guilty, guilty'. Sometimes the anxiety experienced by these mothers reached clinical severity. This raised the question whether mothers of a child with anorexia nervosa would benefit from having an assessment of their own mental health needs.

Additionally, mothers expressed how they felt supported when people close to them showed empathy, but became very frustrated when people demonstrated a lack of understanding of the condition. Fathers, on the other hand, often showed a more cognitive and detached approach to dealing with their child's anorexia nervosa. While the mothers were far more emotionally involved, the fathers were more preoccupied with the effect the illness would have on their child's future. They often felt bewildered by the condition and used a form of wishful thinking to cope with their fears and sense of hopelessness about the future. Fathers, also, tended to use work as a distractor to take their mind off their child's ill-health.

References

Treasure, J., Murphy, T., Szmukler, G., Todd, G., Gavan, K., Joyce, J. 'The Experience of Caregiving for Severe Mental Illness: A Comparison Between Anorexia Nervosa and Psychosis'. *Social Psychiatry and Psychiatric Epidemiology* 36(7) (2001): pp. 343-7.

Appendix 3: Family Impact

Whitney, J., Murray, J., Gavan, K., Todd, G., Whitaker, W., Treasure, J. 'Experience of Caring For Someone With Anorexia Nervosa: Qualitative Study'. *British Journal of Psychiatry* 187 (2005): pp. 444-9.

Appendix 4
Finding Help

This appendix is kindly provided by Beat,
the UK's eating disorder charity.

If you're concerned about yourself or about somebody you know, you are not alone. Eating disorders are treatable, full recovery is possible, and there are so many places you can turn to that will provide support and guidance. It's important to access treatment as early as you can to ensure the best chance of recovery.

Beat, the UK's eating disorder charity, is a champion, guide and friend to anyone affected by these serious mental illnesses. Beat has support services for both people with eating disorders and their loved ones. You can see more information on the services available below.

Helplines
Beat run both an adult helpline and a dedicated youthline for under-18s. Their fully trained staff will listen to your concerns, whether they're about yourself or someone you know, and can signpost you to other places that can help.

The helpline is free to call, including from mobile, and the number won't appear on your phone bill, ensuring confidentiality. They are open 365 days a year from 4pm-10pm.

You can contact the helpline on 0808 801 0677 or email help@b-eat.co.uk. You can call the youthline on 0808 801 0711 or email fyp@b-eat.co.uk.

Message boards

The Beat message boards are for anyone suffering from an eating disorder or their loved ones. They give you the opportunity to talk to and get advice and support from people who are going through or have been through similar experiences.

There are message boards for adults and for under-18s. All messages are carefully moderated prior to posting to ensure that no harmful content or identifying information is shared.

Find out how to access the Beat message boards at www.b-eat.co.uk/support-services/message-boards.

Online support groups

Beat hosts several online support groups. These give you the opportunity to talk to people who have similar experiences, whether you personally have or have had an eating disorder or you're supporting someone who does.

All groups are hosted by a trained member of Beat staff, who will ensure that no harmful content or identifying content is posted.

Find out how to access online support groups at www.b-eat.co.uk/support-services/online-support-groups.

Helpfinder

Beat runs a service, Helpfinder, to help you find support and treatment in your area, including support groups, private clinics, therapists, and more. It also offers more information about treatment so that you have more of an idea about what to expect and can choose the most suitable pathway. Visit helpfinder.b-eat.co.uk.

Information

At www.b-eat.co.uk you can find out lots more information about different types of eating disorder, spotting the early signs and symptoms, what to do if you're concerned, treatment, and much more.

You can also use Beat's range of leaflets, available for download from the website or to order by emailing info@b-eat.co.uk.

Campaigning
Beat runs campaigns to help people with eating disorders get the standard of care they need and deserve as early as possible. To find out more, go to www.b-eat.co.uk/support-us/campaigning.

LETTER TO SOMEONE GOING TO SEE THE DOCTOR

[This letter is available as an A4 download from LifeHurts.net so that you can give it to anyone who is going to see the doctor about an eating disorder]

DR ELIZABETH MᶜNAUGHT

Dear Friend,

I doubt that you want other people interfering in your life, you want to be in control. So please read on and see how you can make your own decisions about your own body.

When you go in to see the doctor you will probably be told what will happen to your body if you keep on with your eating disorder. You might be told about how your bones will weaken, you may become infertile so you can never have children, you may develop diabetes if you are binge eating, and your teeth may decay if you make yourself sick. Of course, you may not have that future, because if you keep living with your eating disorder and not eating properly your heart could stop working and you will suddenly die.

You may not want to listen when your doctor tells you all of this. So, why would you listen to me? Well, I'm not just another doctor, I am someone who has also gone through it myself. I wouldn't listen to my doctor. I wanted to control my own life. But I was kidding myself. I wasn't in control. Anorexia was controlling me, it's like an internal bully that won't leave you alone.

However far you continue with the eating disorder, it won't be enough. You can't eat so little that it will silence the bully enough. You will never be thin enough. You will never be liked enough. But you will damage your life enough to wish that these years had never happened. You will push your friends away enough that you feel you have no-one your own age to turn to. You will damage your family enough that your home will become a battleground where everyone loses.

How I wish I had stood up to that bully and taken back control of my life. How I wish I had not lost all those teenage years when I should have been out having fun. How I wish I had not caused my family so much pain. How I wish I had not let the thought patterns become so fixed in my mind that I couldn't eat.

But you have a choice today.

You can believe the lie of the bully. You can carry on being deceived into thinking that using food, or the avoidance of it, to deal with your emotions puts you in control. Or you can fight back, fight against those lies, and live in the truth. Your family will support you, your true friends will stand with you, the doctors will help you. But it has to begin with you. It's your choice. You can choose to fight as the strong, powerful person you are, or to give in and let the bully of an eating disorder take over your life.

How I wish I could be you again, sat in this waiting room. How I wish I could make that choice again. I'd choose life. I'd choose to fight the thoughts and feelings that made me not want to eat. I'd choose to work with the doctors, not against them.

Well, you have that choice right now. You can tell the doctor that you want to fight for your life. You can ask for help to deal with the reasons why you started wanting to control what you eat, the hurts you've experienced, the way you feel about yourself. You can tell the doctor that meal plans and weight targets will not be enough, and that you need help to deal with the causes not just the symptoms. Perhaps you'll need to fight for this help, because it's not easy for a doctor to ensure you get it. And perhaps that will be your first step of fighting for control of your life.

It's up to you. It's your choice.

 x

Appendix 6
Signs and Symptoms

This list is reprinted here, with kind permission, from the website of Beat, the national eating disorder charity (see www.B-eat.co.uk)

Behavioural signs and symptoms

- Fear of fatness or pursuit of thinness
- Pre-occupation with body weight
- Distorted perception of body shape or weight
- May underestimate the seriousness of the problem even after diagnosis
- May tell lies about eating or what they have eaten, give excuses about why they are not eating, pretend they have eaten earlier
- Not being truthful about how much weight they have lost
- Finding it difficult to think about anything other than food
- Strict dieting
- Counting the calories in food excessively
- Avoiding food they think is fattening
- Eating only low-calorie food
- Missing meals (fasting)
- Avoiding eating with other people
- Hiding food
- Cutting food into tiny pieces – to make it less obvious they have eaten little and to make food easier to swallow
- Taking appetite suppressants, such as slimming or diet pills
- Rigidity
- Obsessive behaviour

- Excessive exercising
- Vomiting or misusing laxatives (purging)
- Social withdrawal and isolation, shutting off from the world
- Compromise of educational and employment plans
- Getting irritable and moody
- Setting high standards and being a perfectionist
- Can be associated with depression and obsessive-compulsive disorder (OCD)

Physical signs and symptoms
- Severe weight loss
- In girls and women, periods stop or are irregular (amenorrhoea)
- Lack of sexual interest or potency
- Difficulty sleeping and tiredness
- Feeling dizzy
- Stomach pains
- Constipation and bloating
- Feeling cold or having a low body temperature
- Growth of downy (soft and fine) hair all over body (called lanugo)
- Hair falls out
- Difficulty concentrating
- Weakness or loss of muscle strength
- Effects on endocrine system
- Swelling in feet, hands or face (known as oedema)
- Low blood pressure